Piano • Vocal • Guitar

WORLD MUSIC SONGBOOK

More Than 100 Folk Songs from Countries Across the Globe

ISBN 978-1-4234-2580-9

HAL•LEONARD®
CORPORATION

7777 W. BLUEMOUND RD. P.O. BOX 13819 MILWAUKEE, WI 53213

In Australia Contact:
Hal Leonard Australia Pty. Ltd.
4 Lentara Court
Cheltenham, Victoria, 3192 Australia
Email: ausadmin@halleonard.com.au

Visit Hal Leonard Online at
www.halleonard.com

INDEX BY TITLE

INDEX BY TITLE

INDEX BY ORIGIN

INDEX BY ORIGIN

A LA NANITA NANA
(Hear Lullabies and Sleep Now)

Traditional Spanish Melody

All the world, lit - tle Sav - ior, Thy prais - es sing - ing,

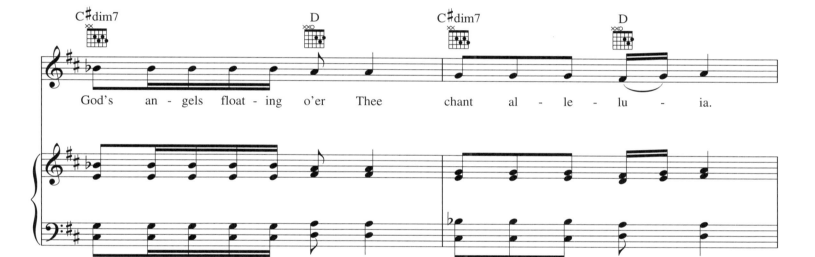

God's an - gels float - ing o'er Thee chant al - le - lu - ia.

A la na - ni - ta na - na, na - ni - ta e - a.

más. A-cu-den a mi men-te re-cuer-dos de o-tros tiem-pos, de los be-llos mo
pre-mo, no hay quien se le re-sis-ta, Ya es-toy a-cos-tum-

men-tos que an-ta-ño dis-fru-té. cer-qui-ta de mi ma-dre, san-ta vie-
bra-do, su ley a res-pe-tar, pues mi vi-da des-hi-zo con sus man-

ji-ta, y de mi no-vie-ci-ta, que tan-to i-do-la-tré. Se a-cuer-dan que e-ra her-
da-tos lle-ván-do-me a mi ma-dre y a mi no-via tam-bién. Dos lá-gri-mas sin-

mo-sa, más lin-da que u-na di-o-sa, y que bri-o-so
ce-ras de-rra-mo en mi par-ti-da por la ba-rra que-

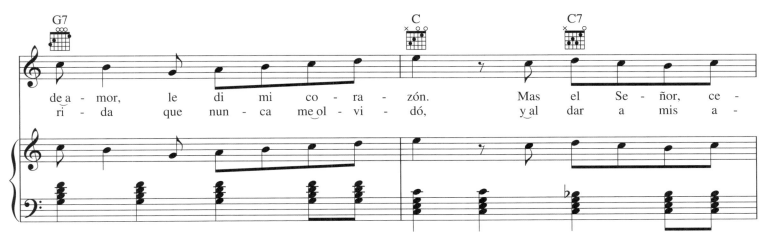

de a - mor, le di mi co - ra - zón. Mas el Se - ñor, ce -
ri - da que nun - ca me ol - vi - dó, y al dar a mis a -

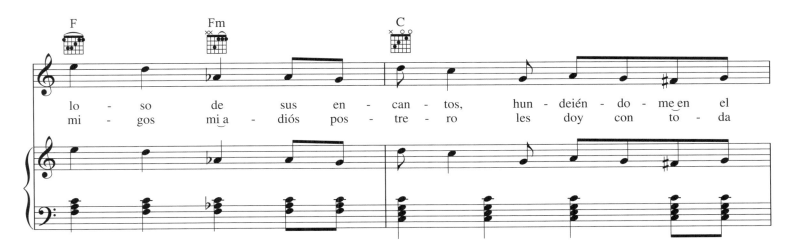

lo - so de sus en - can - tos, hun - deién - do - me en el
mi - gos mi a - diós pos - tre - ro les doy con to - da

llan - to se la lle - vó. Es Dios el juez su -
mi al - ma, mi ben - di - ción. A - diós mu -

cuer - po en - fer - mo no re - sis - te más.

moun - tain, o - ver the hills and ev - 'ry - where. ___

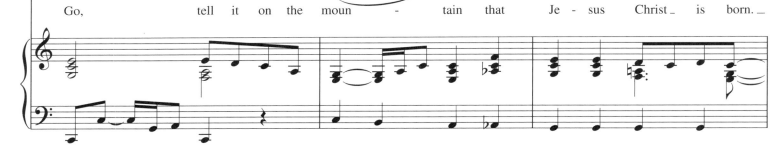

Go, tell it on the moun - tain that Je - sus Christ _ is born. _

The __ Je - sus Christ _ is born!
Down

Sing we all no - el.

Sing we all no - el.　　　　Sing we all no - el.　　　　Sing we all no - el!

ACH, DU LIEBER AUGUSTIN
(O My Dearest Augustine)

18th Century German Folk Song

AH, POOR BIRD

Traditional

AIJA, ANZIT, AIJA
(Lullaby)

Latvian Folk Song

ALL THROUGH THE NIGHT

Welsh Folk Song

Sleep, my Child, and peace at-tend Thee, All through the
While the moon her peace watch is keep - ing, All through the

night;
night;
Guard - ian an - gels God will send Thee,
While the wea - ry world is sleep - ing,

All through the night.
All through the night.
Soft the drows - y
Through your dreams you're

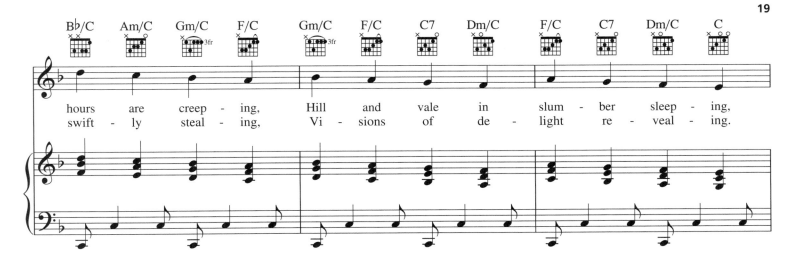

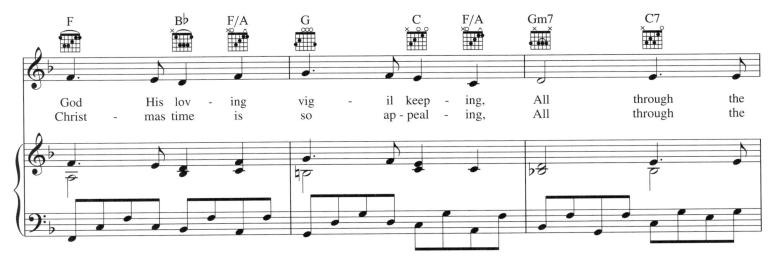

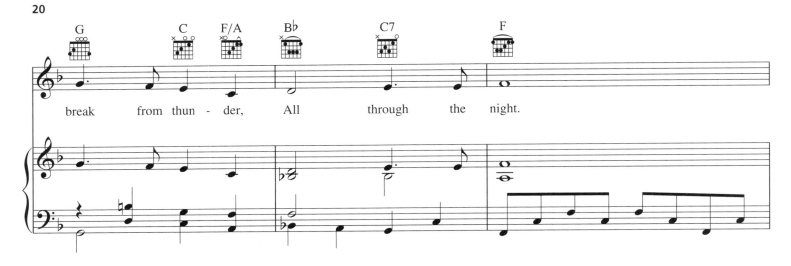

break from thun - der, All through the night.

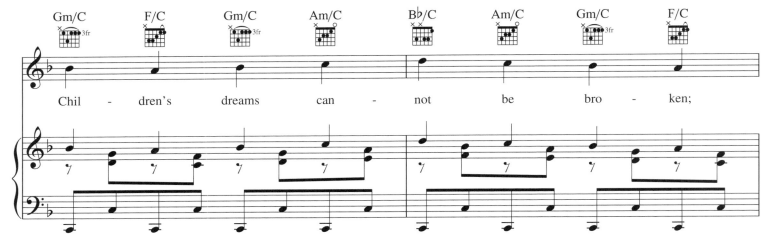

Chil - dren's dreams can - not be bro - ken;

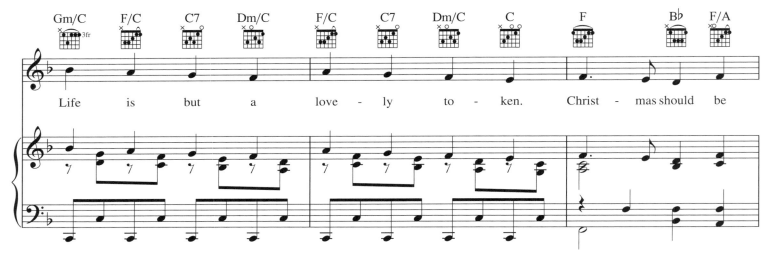

Life is but a love - ly to - ken. Christ - mas should be

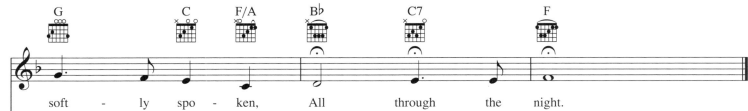

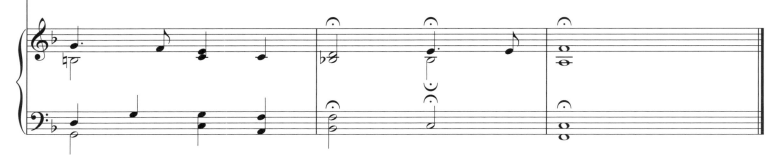

soft - ly spo - ken, All through the night.

ALOHA OE

Words and Music by
QUEEN LILIUOKALANI

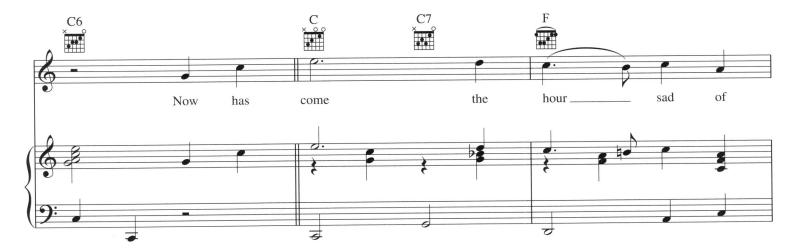

Now has come the hour _____ sad of

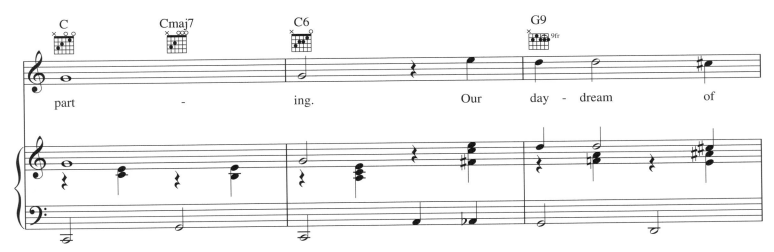

part - ing. Our day - dream of

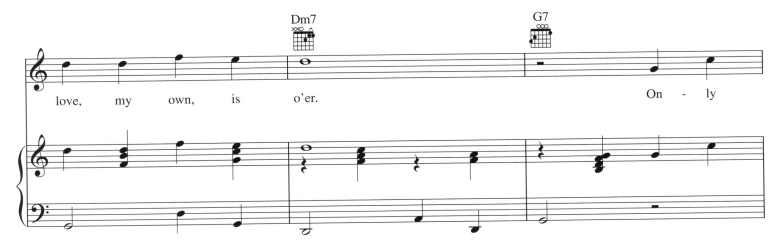

love, my own, is o'er. On - ly

mem - o - ries will soon be left

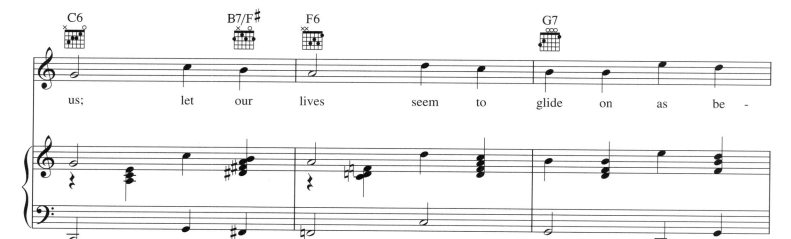

us; let our lives seem to glide on as be -

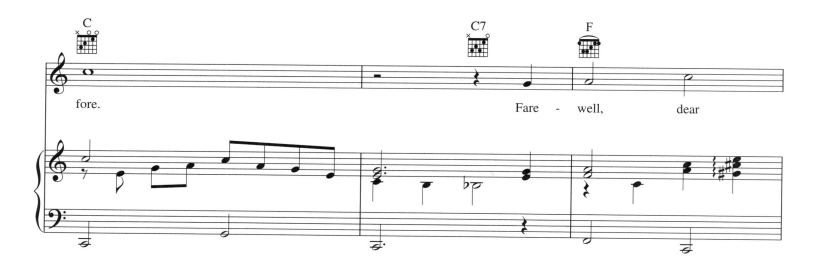

fore. Fare - well, dear

love, I'll dream of you. No

pass - ing grief is this my heart is feel -

ing. I love you so; be -

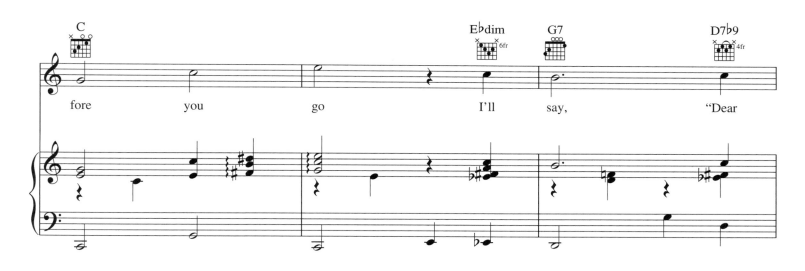

fore you go I'll say, "Dear

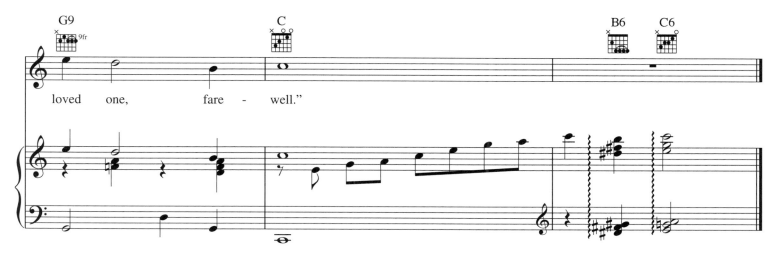

loved one, fare - well."

AU CLAIR DE LA LUNE

French Folk Song

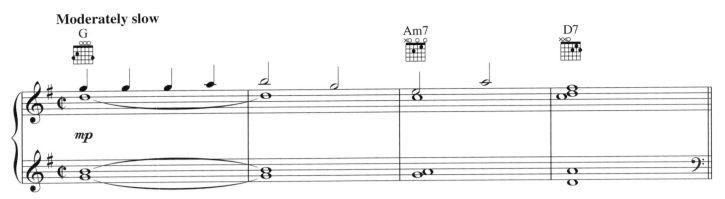

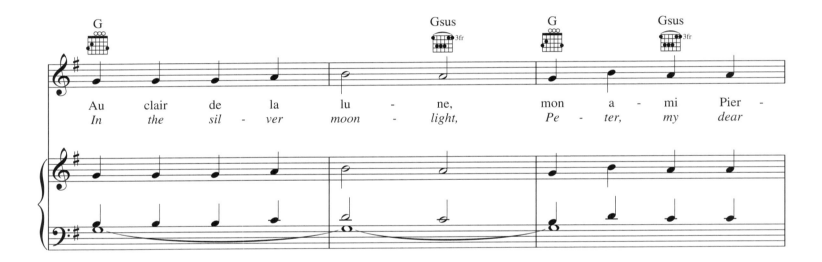

Au clair de la lu - ne, mon a - mi Pier -
In the sil - ver moon - light, Pe - ter, my dear

rot,   prê - te moi ta plu - me
friend,   please lend me your pen - cil

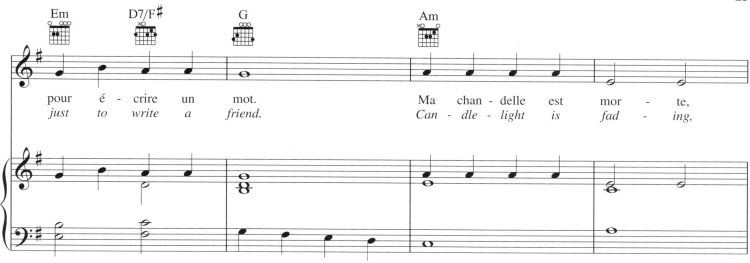

pour é - crire un mot.
just to write a friend.

Ma chan - delle est mor - te,
Can - dle - light is fad - ing,

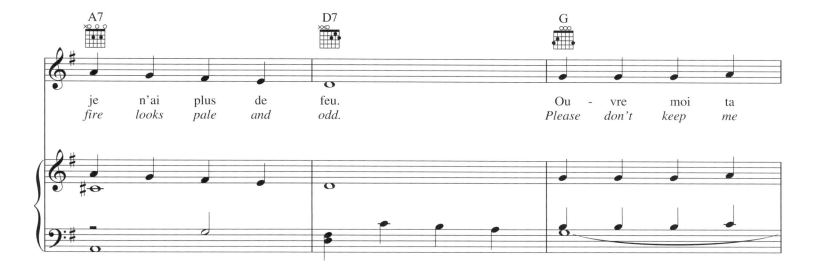

je n'ai plus de feu.
fire looks pale and odd.

Ou - vre moi ta
Please don't keep me

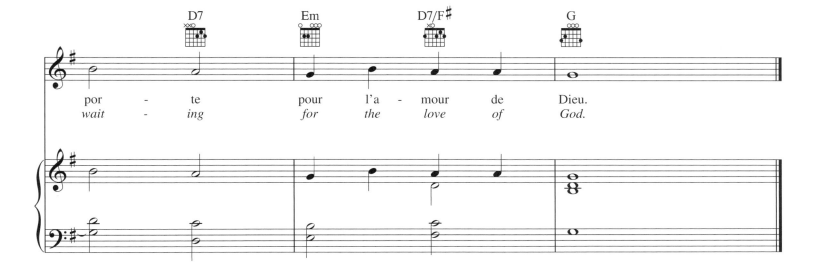

por - te pour l'a - mour de Dieu.
wait - ing for the love of God.

BALLAD OF NED KELLY

19th Century Australian

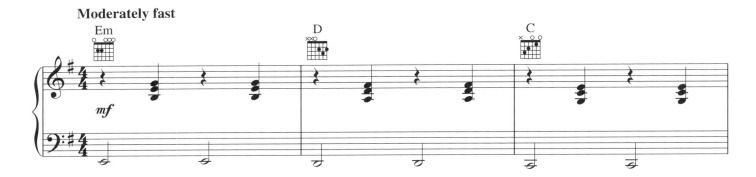

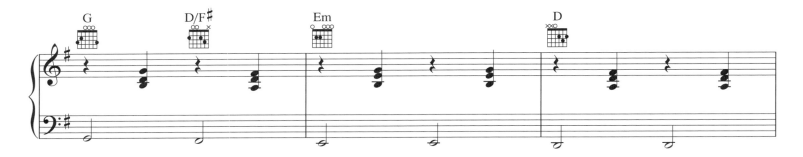

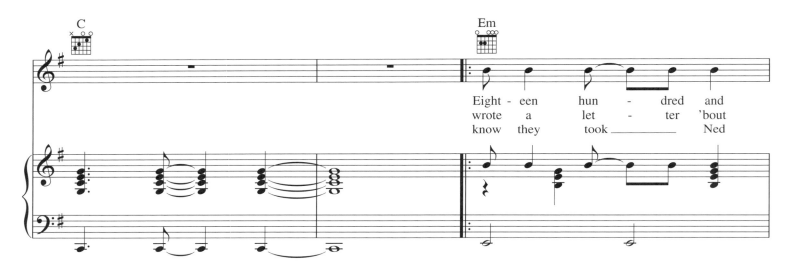

Eight - een hun - dred and
wrote a let - ter 'bout
know they took _____ Ned

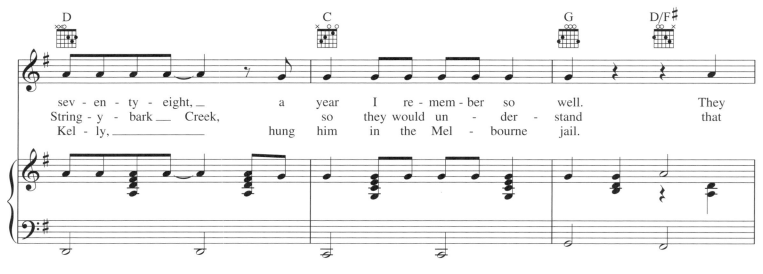

sev - en - ty - eight, ___ a year I re - mem - ber so well. They
String - y - bark ___ Creek, so they would un - der - stand that
Kel - ly, _____ hung him in the Mel - bourne jail.

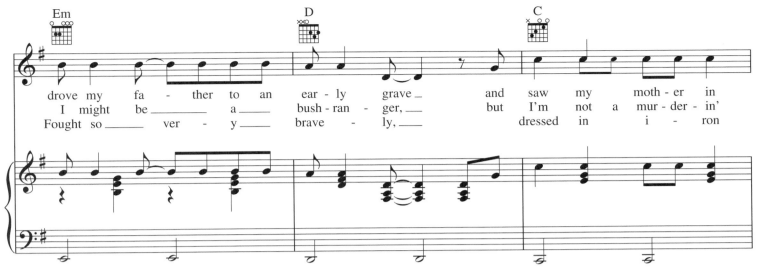

Em / D / C

drove my fa - ther to an ear - ly grave ___ and saw my moth - er in
I might be ___ a ___ bush - ran - ger, ___ but I'm not a mur - der - in'
Fought so ___ ver - y ___ brave - ly, ___ dressed in i - ron

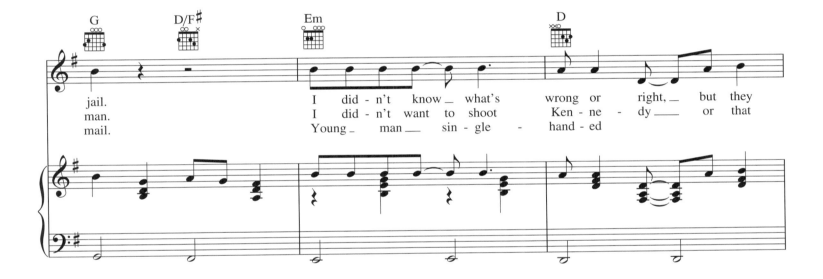

G / D/F# / Em / D

jail. I did - n't know ___ what's wrong or right, ___ but they
man. I did - n't want to shoot Ken - ne - dy ___ or that
mail. Young ___ man ___ sin - gle - hand - ed

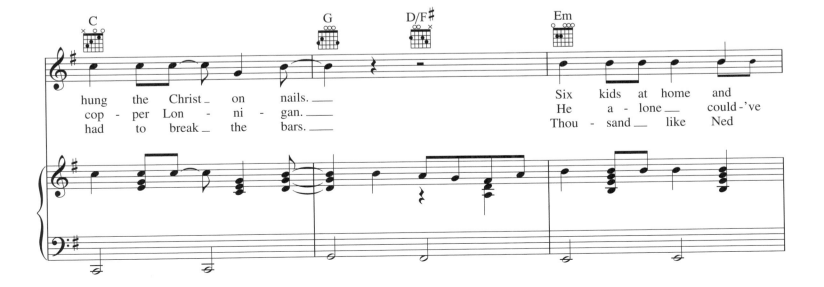

C / G / D/F# / Em

hung the Christ ___ on nails. ___ Six kids at home and
cop - per Lon - ni - gan. ___ He a - lone ___ could -'ve
had to break ___ the bars. ___ Thou - sand ___ like Ned

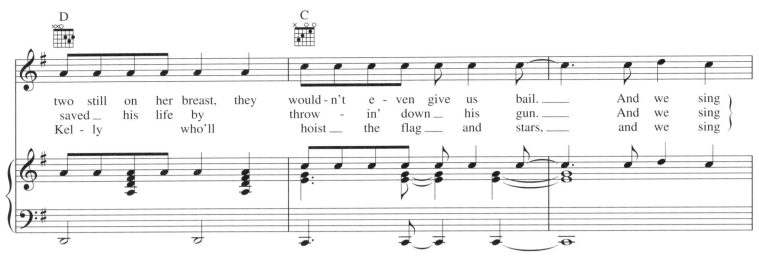

two still on her breast, they would -n't e - ven give us bail. _____ And we sing
saved _ his life by throw - in' down _ his gun. _____ And we sing
Kel - ly who'll hoist _ the flag _ and stars, _____ and we sing

Poor Ned, you're bet - ter off dead, at least you get some peace of

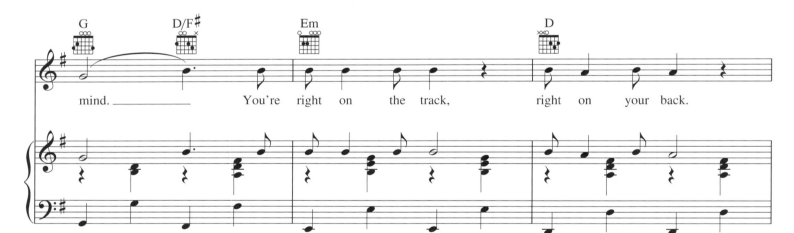

mind. _____ You're right on the track, right on your back.

Boy, they're gon - na hang you high. ____ Well, I
Well, you

ALOUETTE

Traditional

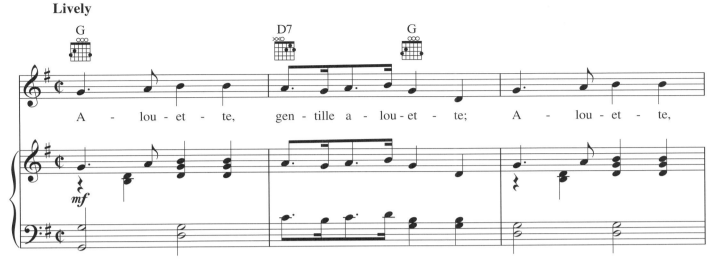

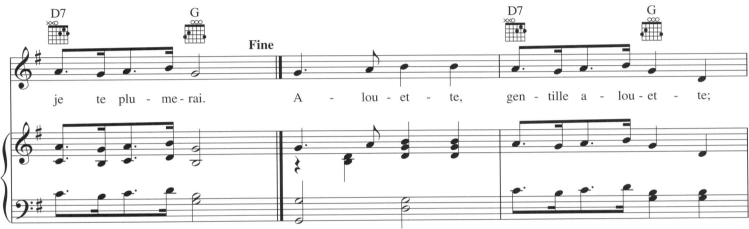

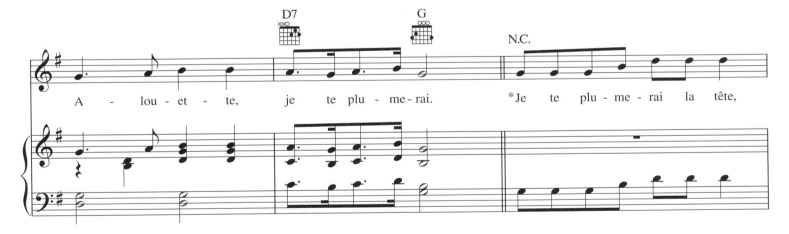

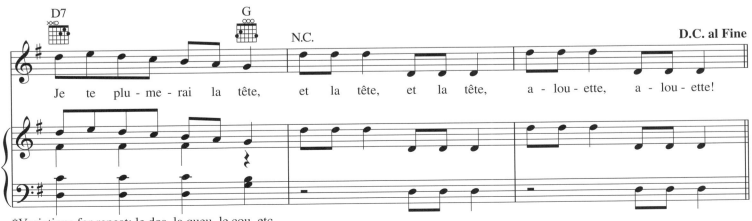

*Variations for repeat: le dos, la queue, le cou, etc.

THE BAMBOO FLUTE

Chinese Folk Song

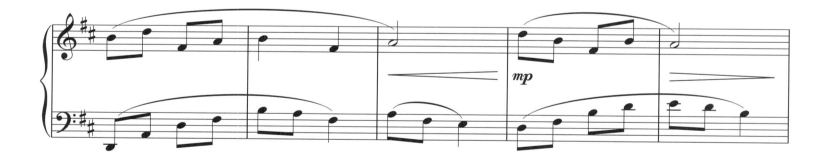

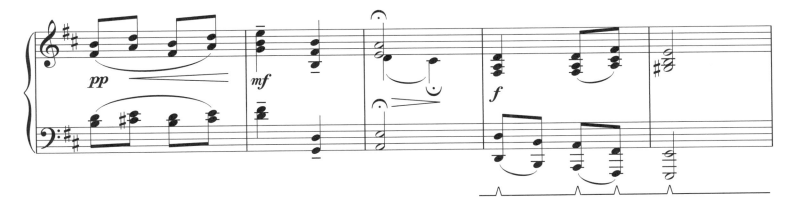

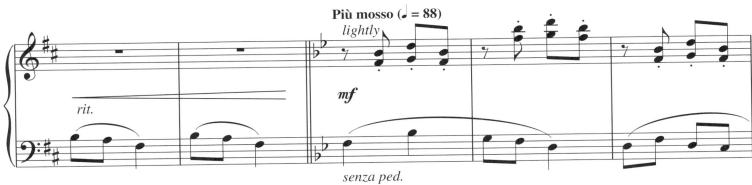

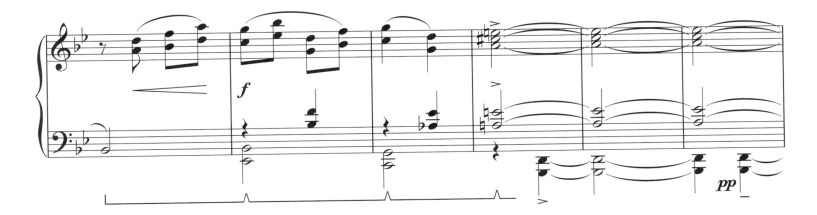

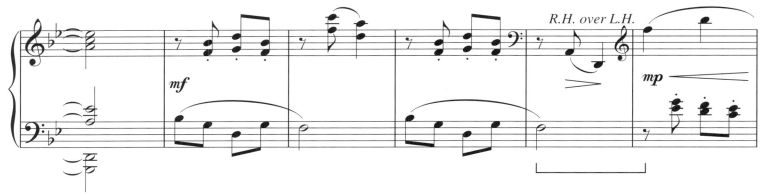

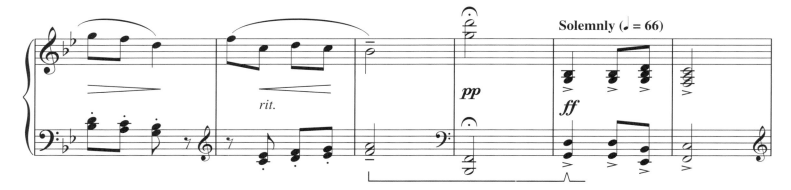

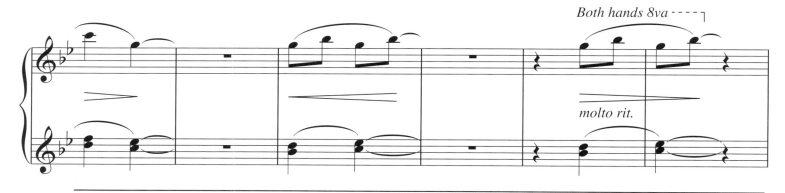

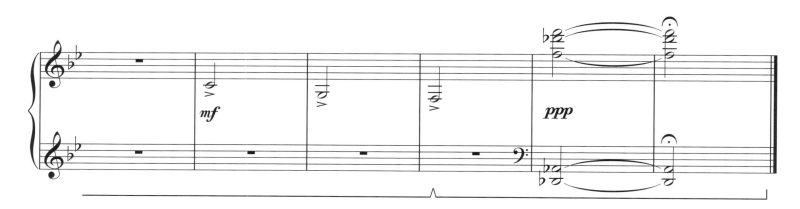

THE BANANA BOAT SONG

Jamaican Work Song

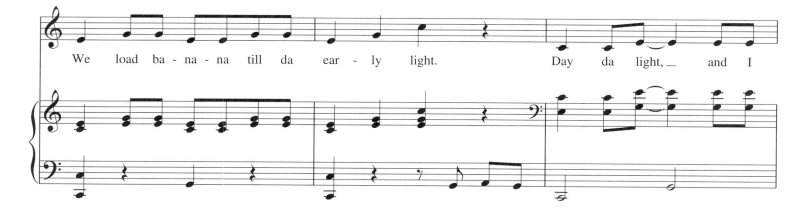

We load ba-na-na till da ear-ly light. Day da light, ___ and I

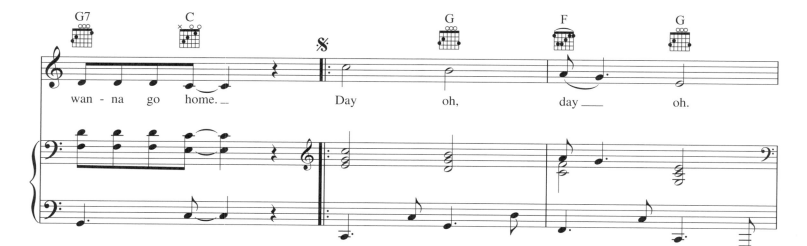

wan-na go home. ___ Day oh, day ___ oh.

Day da light, ___ and I wan-na go home. ___

Come, Mis-ter Tal-ly-man, come tal-ly me ba-na-na. Day da light, ___ and I

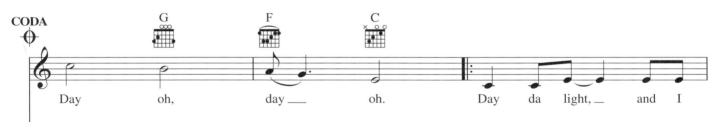

THE BANKS OF THE DON

Traditional

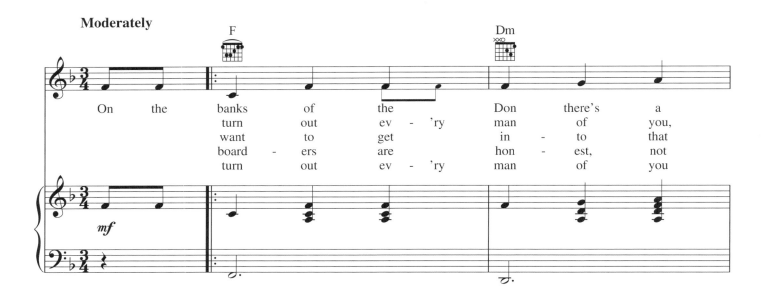

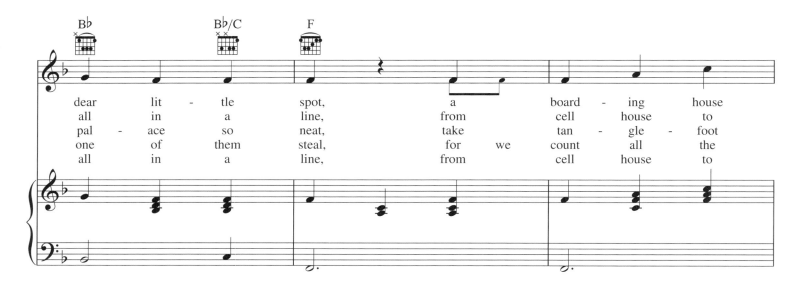

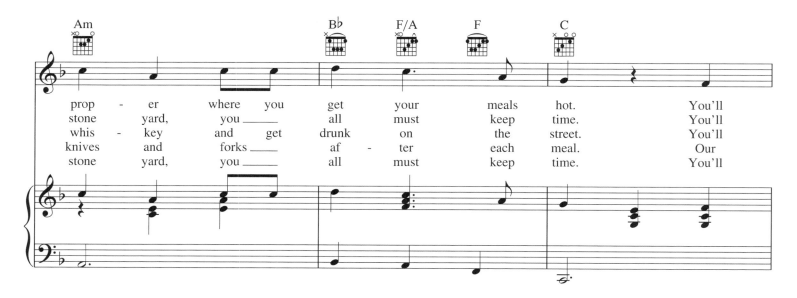

THE BLOOMING BRIGHT STAR OF BELLE ISLE

Traditional

One eve-ning for pleas-ure I
spied a fair maid at her
hum-bled my-self to her

ram-bled, __ to __ view the fair fields all a - lone; __ down __ by __ the banks of Loch
la-bor, __ which __ caused me to stay for a while; __ I __ thought her the god-dess of
beau-ty. __ "Fair maid-en, where do you be - long? __ Are __ you from the heav-ens de -

E - rin, where __ beau-ty and __ pleas-ure were known. I
beau-ty, the __ bloom-ing bright star of Belle Isle. I
scend - ed, a - bid-ing in __ Cu-pid's fair throng?"

THE BLUE BELLS OF SCOTLAND

Words and Music attributed to
MRS. JORDON

BOIL THEM CABBAGE DOWN

American Folk Song

Moderately fast Bluegrass

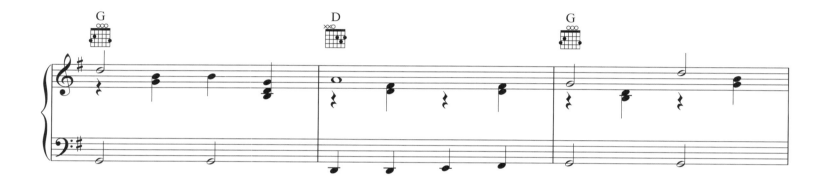

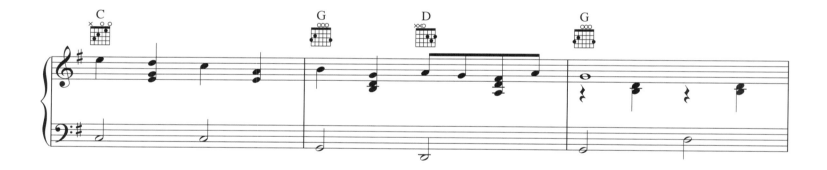

Bile them cab - bage down,

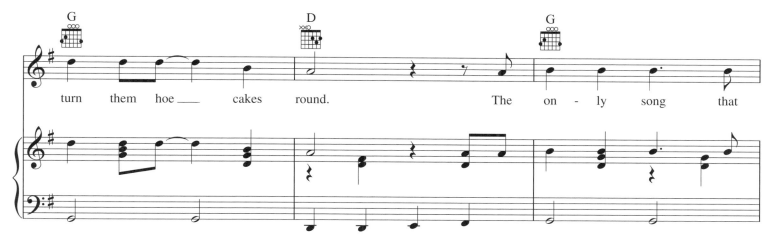

turn them hoe ___ cakes round. The on - ly song that

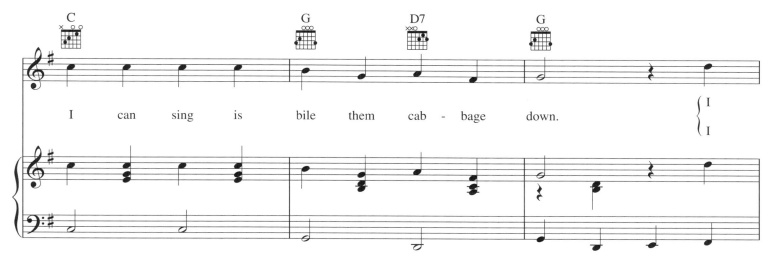

I can sing is bile them cab - bage down.

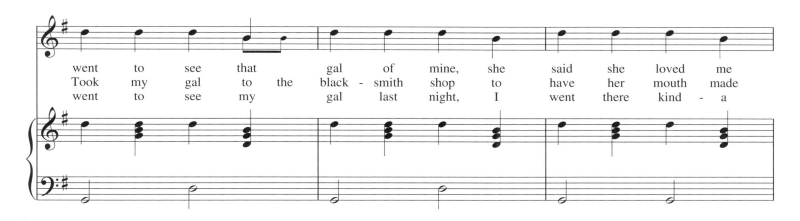

went to see that gal of mine, she said she loved me
Took my gal to the black - smith shop to have her mouth made
went to see my gal last night, I went there kind - a

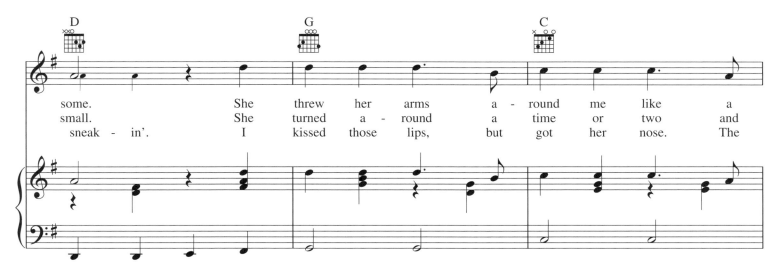

some. She threw her arms a - round me like a
small. She turned a - round a time or two and
sneak - in'. I kissed those lips, but got her nose. The

bind - ing 'round a gun.
swal - lowed shop and all.
whole darn thing was leak - in'.

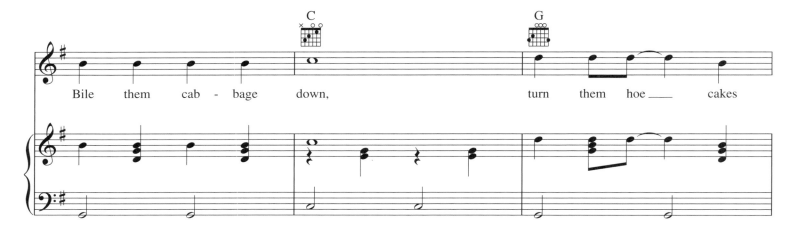

Bile them cab - bage down, turn them hoe ___ cakes

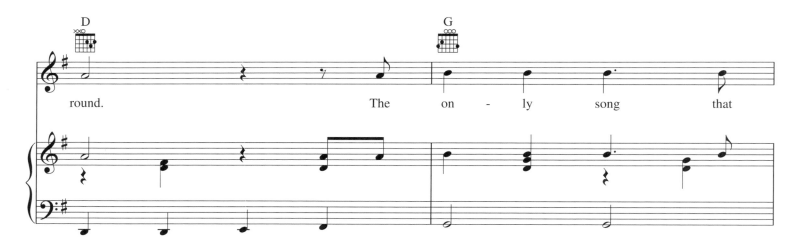

round. The on - ly song that

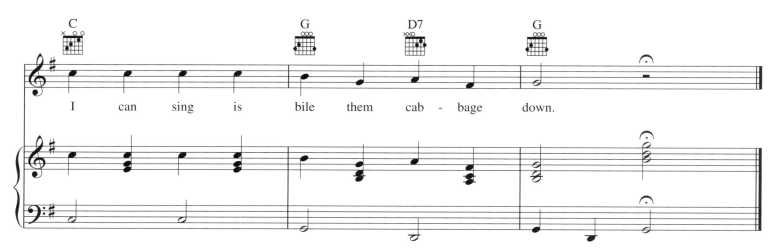

I can sing is bile them cab - bage down.

BOTANY BAY

Australian Folk Song

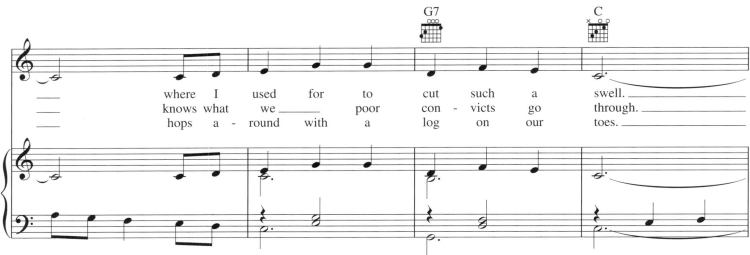

where I used for to cut such a swell. ___
knows what we ___ poor con-victs go through. ___
hops a-round with a log on our toes. ___

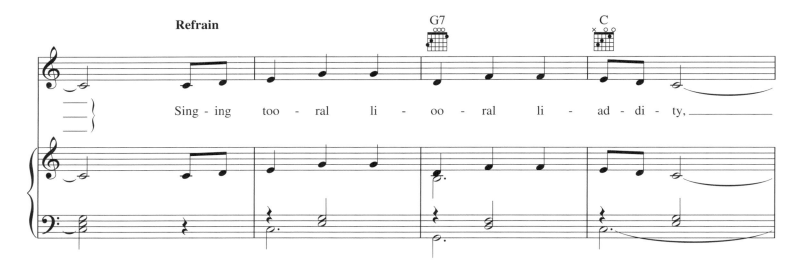

Refrain

Sing-ing too-ral li-oo-ral li-ad-di-ty, ___

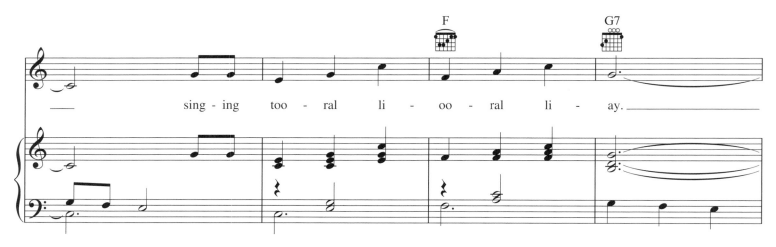

sing-ing too-ral li-oo-ral li-ay. ___

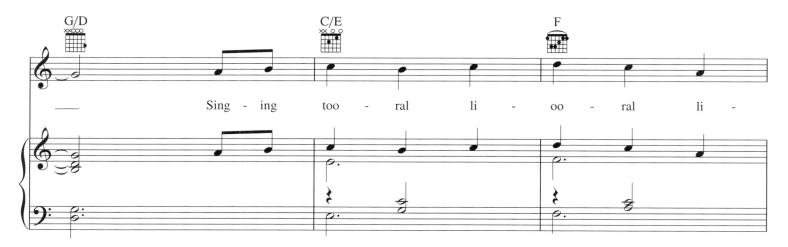

Sing-ing too-ral li-oo-ral li-

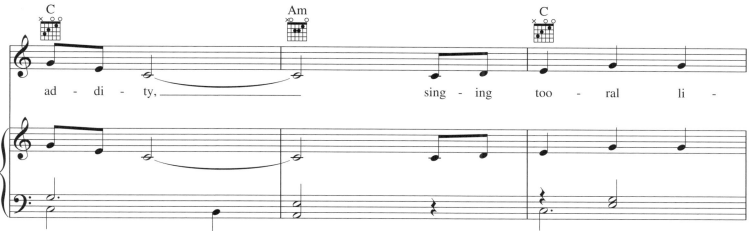

ad - di - ty, _____ sing - ing too - ral li -

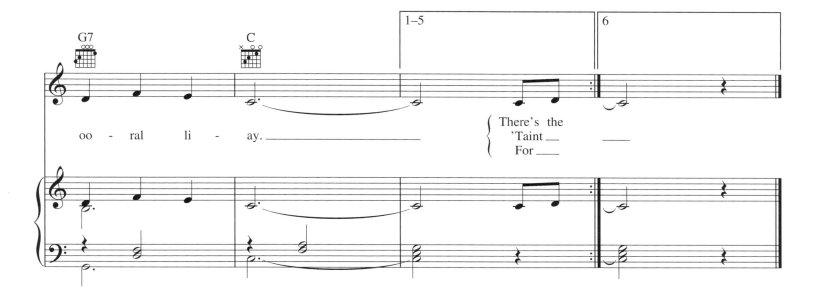

oo - ral li - ay. _____

There's the
'Taint ___ ___
For ___

Additional Lyrics

4. For seven long years I'll be staying here,
   For seven long years and a day.
   For meeting a cove in an area
   And taking his ticker away.
   Refrain

5. Oh, had I the wings of a turtle dove!
   I'd soar on my pinions so high.
   Slap bang to the arms of my Polly love,
   And in her sweet presence I'd die.
   Refrain

6. Now, all my young Dookies and Duchesses,
   Take warning from what I've to say.
   Mind all is your own as you touchesses.
   Or you'll find us in Botany Bay.
   Refrain

BOW AND BALANCE

Traditional

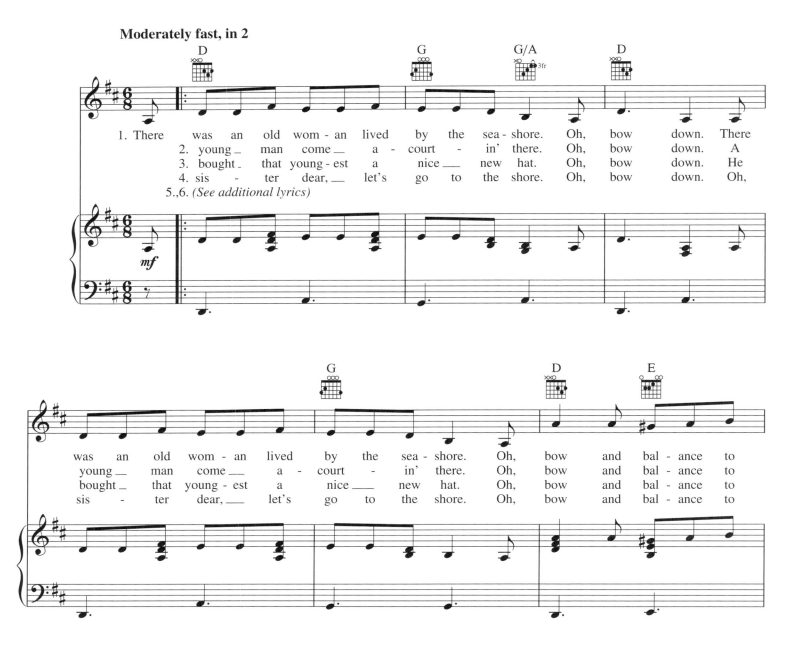

Moderately fast, in 2

1. There was an old wom-an lived by the sea-shore. Oh, bow down. There
2. young _ man come _ a - court - in' there. Oh, bow down. A
3. bought _ that young-est a nice _ new hat. Oh, bow down. He
4. sis - ter dear, _ let's go to the shore. Oh, bow down. Oh,
5.,6. *(See additional lyrics)*

was an old wom-an lived by the sea-shore. Oh, bow and bal-ance to
young _ man come _ a - court - in' there. Oh, bow and bal-ance to
bought _ that young-est a nice _ new hat. Oh, bow and bal-ance to
sis - ter dear, _ let's go to the shore. Oh, bow and bal-ance to

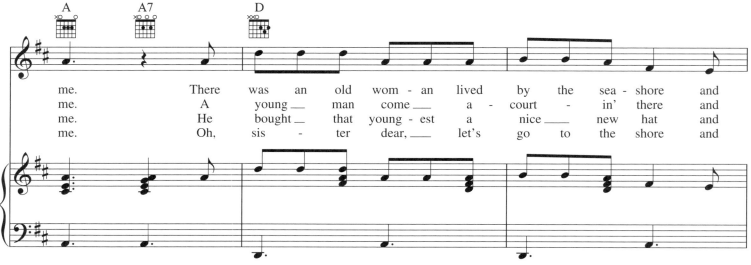

me. There was an old wom-an lived by the sea-shore and
me. A young _ man come _ a - court - in' there and
me. He bought _ that young-est a nice _ new hat and
me. Oh, sis - ter dear, _ let's go to the shore and

Chorus

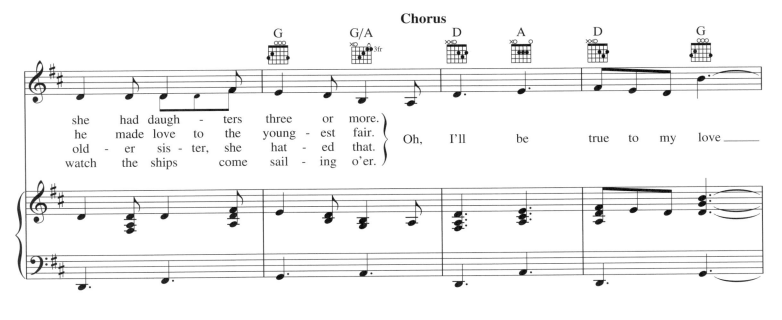

she   had   daugh - ters   three   or   more.
he   made   love   to   the   young - est   fair.
old - er   sis - ter,   she   hat - ed   that.
watch   the   ships   come   sail - ing   o'er.

Oh,   I'll   be   true   to   my   love _____

1–5   **6**

_____   if   my   love   be   true   to   me.

A
He   me.
Oh,

Additional Lyrics

5. And as they walked along the sea rim,
Oh, bow down,
And as they walked along the sea rim,
Oh, bow and balance to me,
And as they walked along the sea rim,
The oldest she pushed the youngest in.
Chorus

6. Oh, sister dear, come lend me your hand,
Oh bow down,
Oh, sister dear, come lend me your hand,
Oh, bow and balance to me.
Oh, sister dear, come lend me your hand
And you can have my house and land.
Chorus

BRING A TORCH, JEANNETTE, ISABELLA

17th Century French Provençal Carol

Brightly

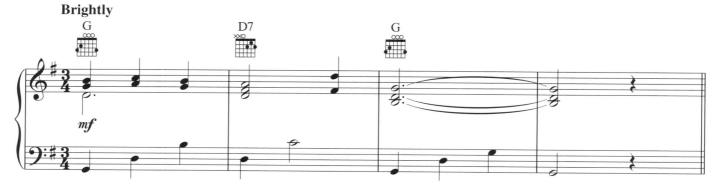

Bring a torch, _____ Jean- nette, Is- a- bel- la,
Has- ten now, _____ good folk of the vil- lage,

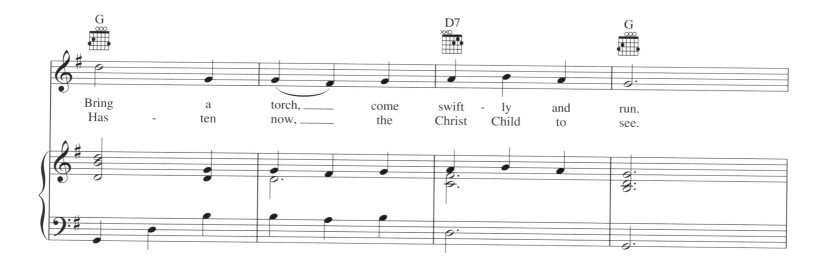

Bring a torch, _____ come swift- ly and run.
Has- ten now, _____ the Christ Child to see.

Christ is born; tell the folk of the vil - lage.
You will find Him a - sleep in a man - ger.

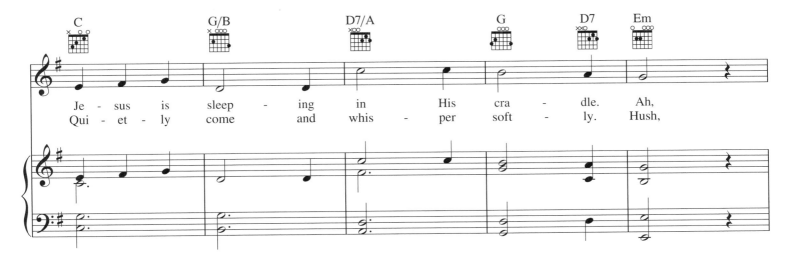

Je - sus is sleep - ing in His cra - dle. Ah,
Qui - et - ly come and whis - per soft - ly. Hush,

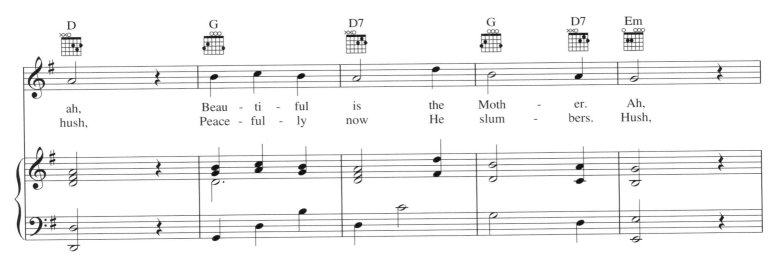

ah, Beau - ti - ful is the Moth - er. Ah,
hush, Peace - ful - ly now He slum - bers. Hush,

ah, Beau - ti - ful is her Son.
hush, Peace - ful - ly now He sleeps.

CAROL OF THE BAGPIPERS

Traditional Sicilian Carol

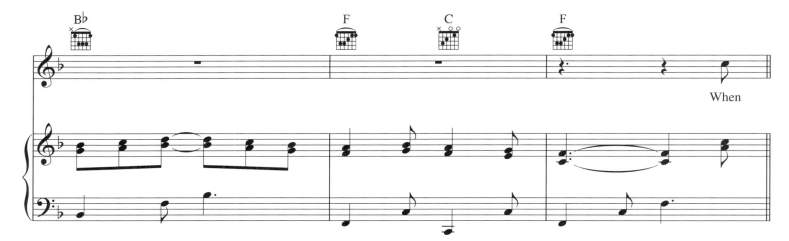

When

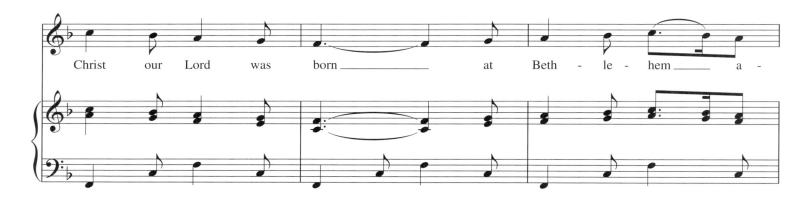

Christ our Lord was born _____ at Beth - le - hem _____ a-

far, _____ al - though 'twas night, there shone _____ as

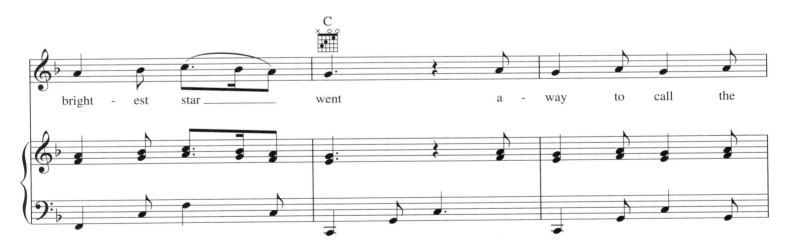

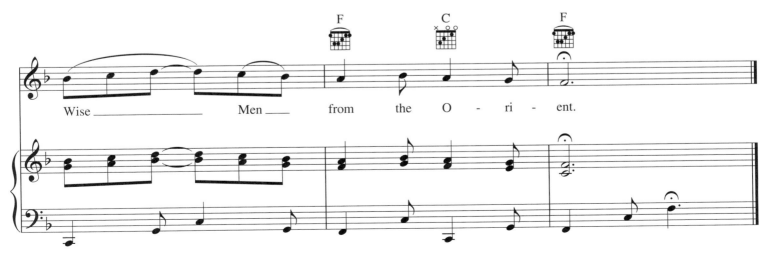

CARNIVAL OF VENICE

By JULIUS BENEDICT

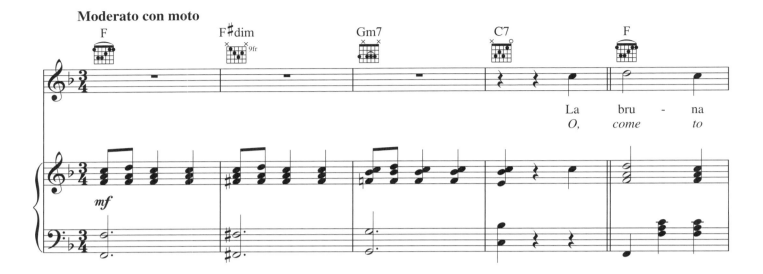

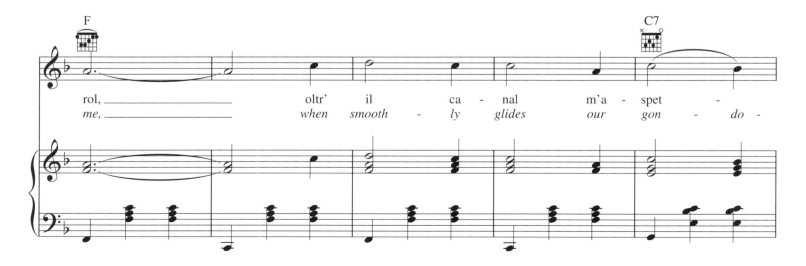

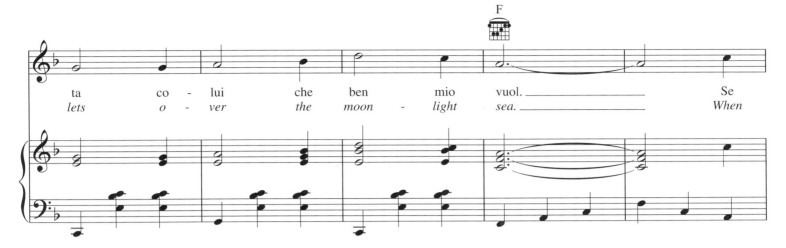

ta co - lui che ben mio vuol. _____ Se
lets o - ver the moon - light sea. _____ When

co - sa e a - mor _____ tu sa - i Deh _____ vie - ni
mirth's _ a - wake _____ and love be - gins be - neath that

non tar - dar. _____ E quel _____ che tu _____ vor -
shin - ing ray, _____ with sounds of gui - tars _____ and

ra - i Prom - et to a te _____ do - nar. _____
man - do - lins to steal young hearts _____ a - way. _____

CHIAPANECAS

Mexican Folk Song

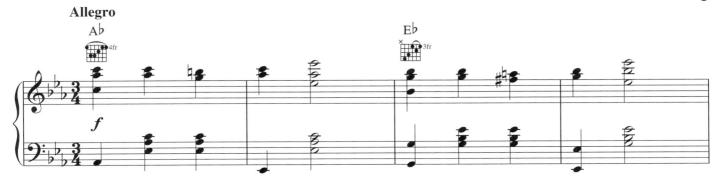

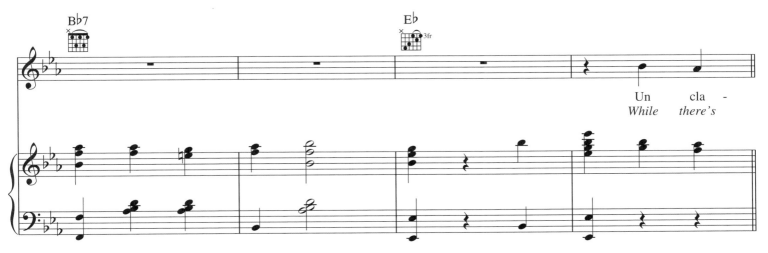

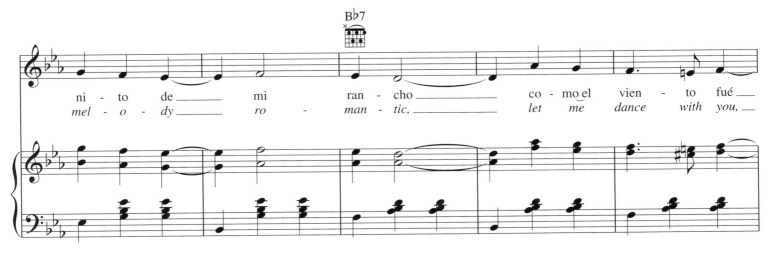

_____ mi ca - ba - llo fiel _____ á lle - var - me has - ta _____
_____ till the night is through. _____ While there's mu - sic there's _____

Eb

_____ su la - do _____ Lin - da flor de a - bril _____
_____ ro - mance. _____ 'Round and 'round we'll glide, _____

Eb7

_____ to - ma es - te cla - vel _____ que te brin - do con _____
_____ while my eyes con - fide _____ love is hid - ing in _____

Ab

_____ pa - sion _____ no me di - gas no _____
_____ their glance. _____ Though the mo - ments fly, _____

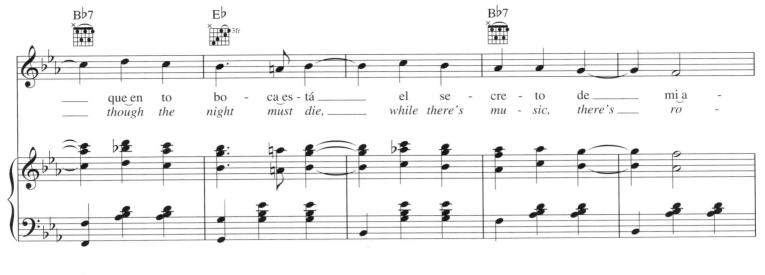

que en to bo- ca es- tá _____ el se- cre- to de _____ mi a-
though the night must die, _____ while there's mu- sic, there's _____ ro-

mor.
mance!

Cuan- do la no- che lle-
Two hearts in rhyme while they

gó
play,

y con su man- to de a-
two hearts in rhyme while we

zul
sway,

el blan- co ran- cho cu-
now is the time to be

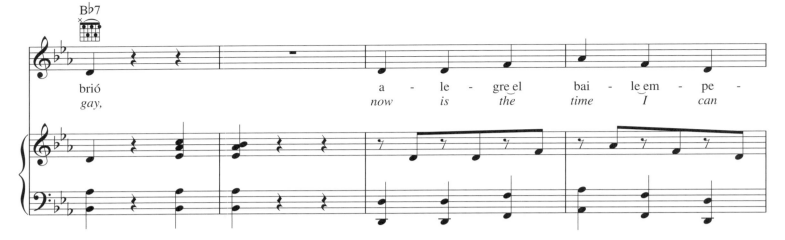

brió
gay,
a - le - gre el bai - le em - pe -
now is the time I can

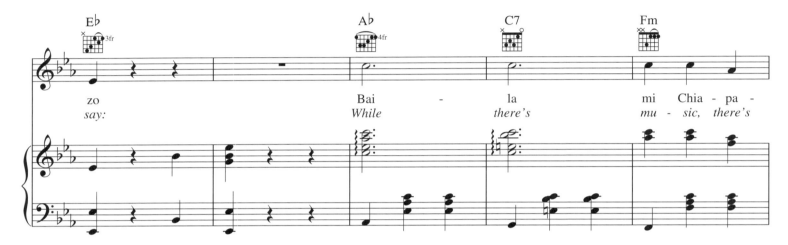

zo
say:
Bai - la
While there's
mi Chia - pa -
mu - sic, there's

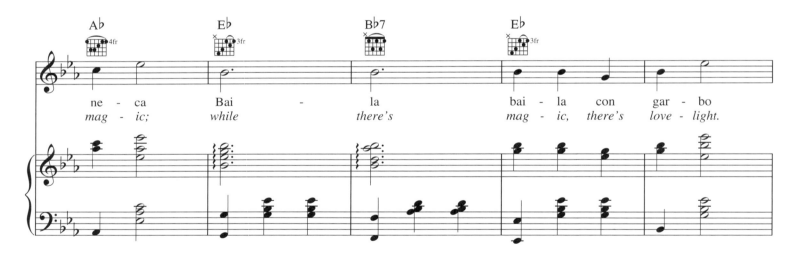

ne - ca
mag - ic;
Bai - la
while there's
bai - la con gar - bo
mag - ic, there's love - light.

Bai - la
In this
sua - ve ra - yo de luz
love - light my heart has a chance

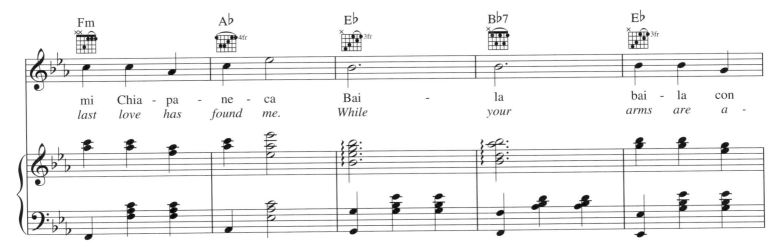

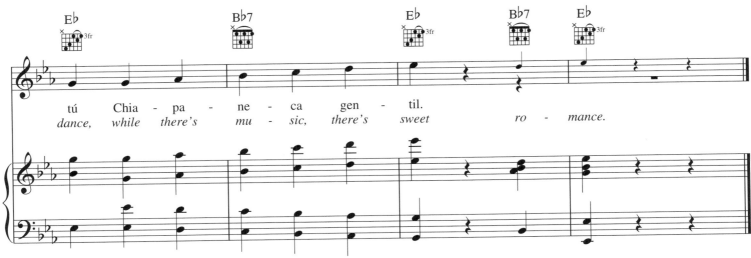

CHOUCOUNE

Haitian Folksong

Moderate Merengue Tempo

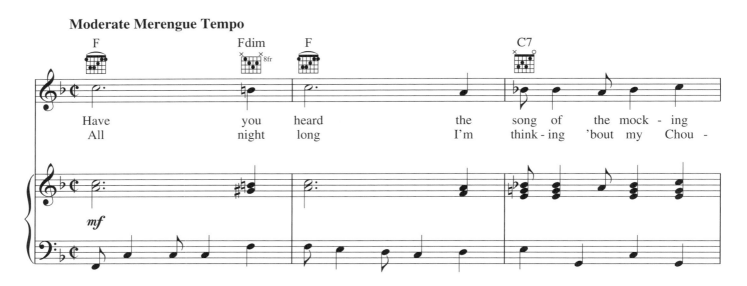

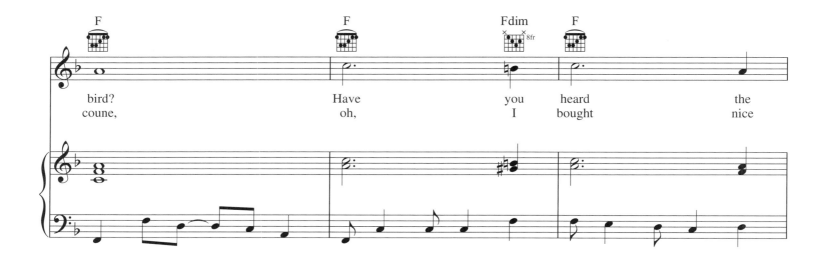

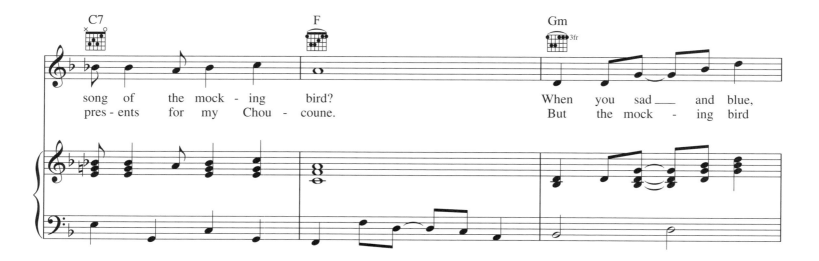

then he mock ___ at you, he sing high ___ a - bove,
says oh have ___ you heard, he, she, she go ___ and fly

and he laugh ___ at love. Oh, I heard ___ his tune
with an - oth - er guy. Morn - ing, night, ___ or noon,

by the Hai - tian moon, when I lost ___ my Chou - coune.
won't she come ___ back soon? I still love ___ my Chou - coune.

CIELITO LINDO
(My Pretty Darling)

By C. FERNANDEZ

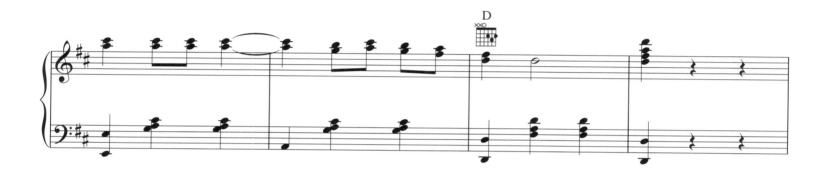

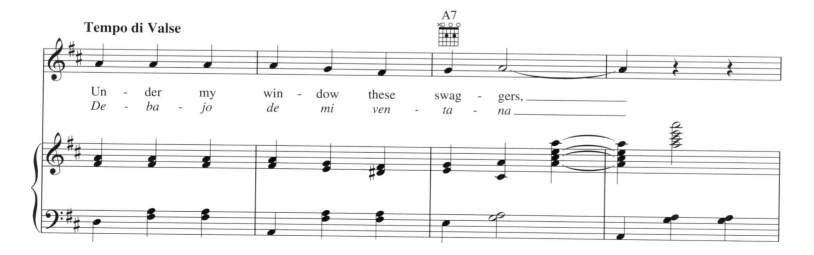

Under my window these swag - gers, _____

De - ba - jo de mi ven - ta - na _____

D

care - less of night and its dag - gers, _____ a char -
pa - sa las no - ches ron - dan - do _____ un cha -

D♯dim **A7**

ri - to,* reck - less fel - low, _____ with a
rri - to muy va - lien - te _____ que me es -

D

plain - tive voice and mel - low. _____
tá a mi e - na - mo - ran - do. _____

A7

Char - ro** who stops at my grat - ing, _____
Ay cha - rri - to no me ron - des _____

* *diminutive of Charro*
** *a rustic swain*

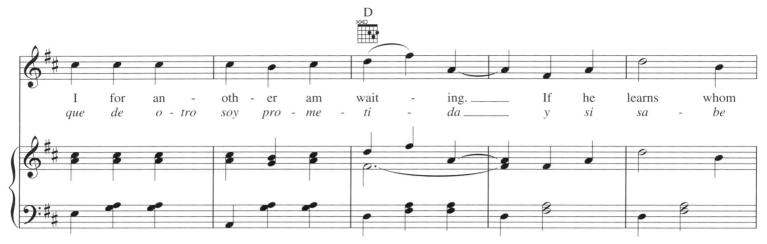

I for an-oth-er am wait - ing.____ If he learns whom
que de o - tro soy pro - me - ti - da____ y si sa - be

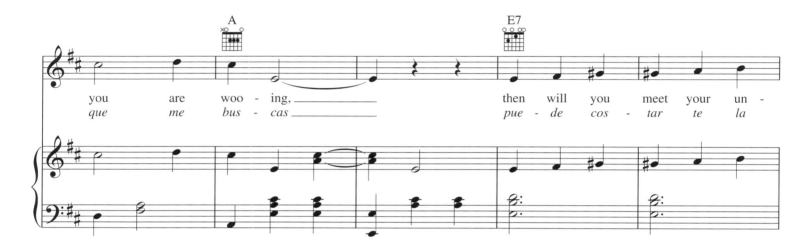

you are woo-ing,_____ then will you meet your un-
que me bus - cas_____ pue - de cos - tar te la

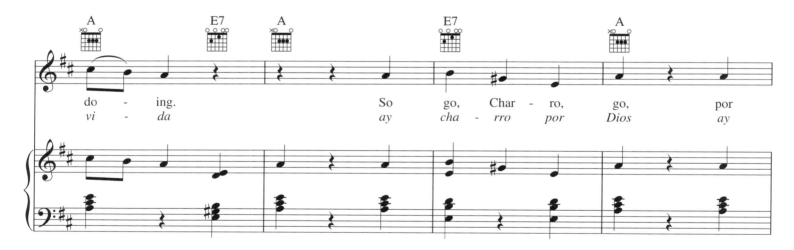

do - ing. So go, Char-ro, go, por
vi - da ay cha - rro por Dios ay

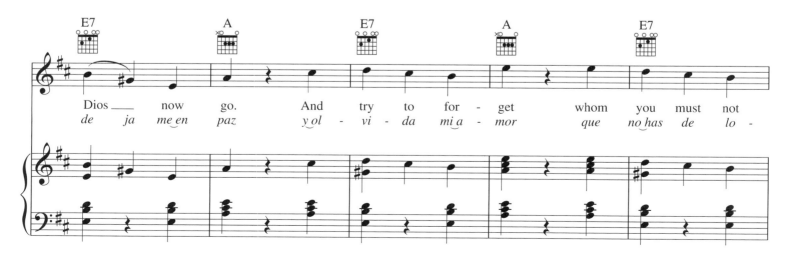

Dios __ now go. And try to for-get whom you must not
de ja me en paz Y ol - vi - da mi a - mor que no has de lo -

know. _____ I love a man from fair Coa-
grar _____ *por que yo quie - ro á u - no de Coa-*

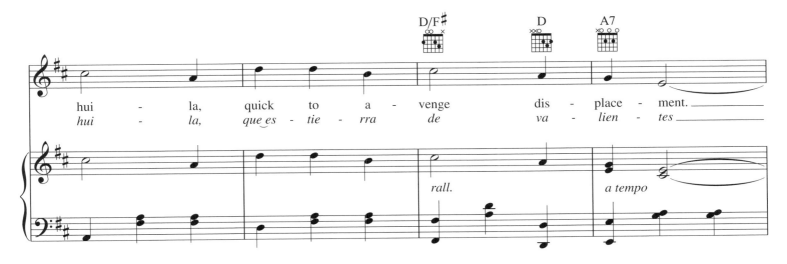

hui - la, quick to a - venge dis - place - ment. _____
hui - la, que es - tie - rra de va - lien - tes _____

_____ Swift - ly he wreaks ef - face - ment _____
que cor un be - so mi al - ma me _____

_____ on a loit - er - er _____ at my case - ment. _____
da la di cha ro - ba mi cal - ma. _____

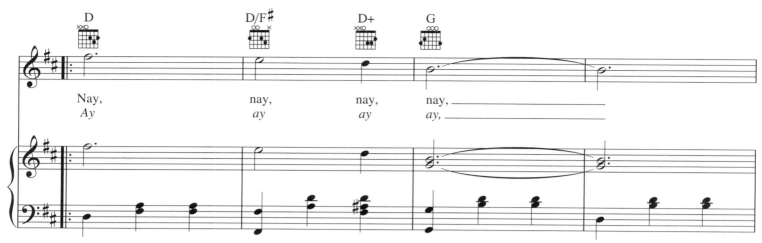

Nay, nay, nay, nay, _____
Ay *ay* *ay* *ay,* _____

seek not my win - dow. _____ For some - where
pier - *de i* - *lu* - *sio* - *nes* _____ *por* *que a* *where* *tu*

some - one will cher - ish you _____ and your pas - sions, Cie -
la - *do* *se a* - *le* - *gran* *cie* - *li* - *to* *lin* - *do* *los* _____

- li - to Lin - do! _____
_____ *co* - *ra* - *zo* - *nes.* _____

CIRANDEIRO

Brazilian Folk Song

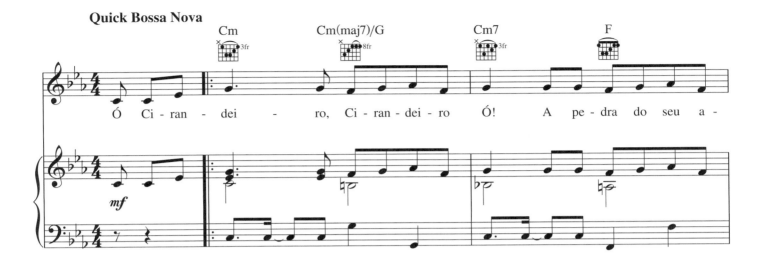

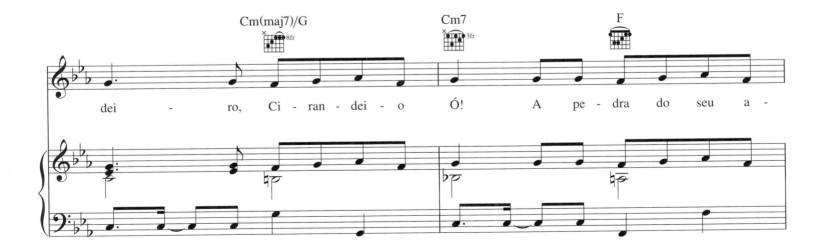

nei bri - lha mais do que o sol!

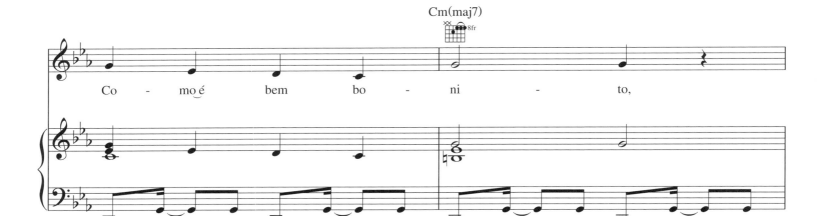

Co - mo é bem bo - ni - to,

meu a - mor can - tar!

A ci - ran - da gi - ra! Ó Ci - ran -

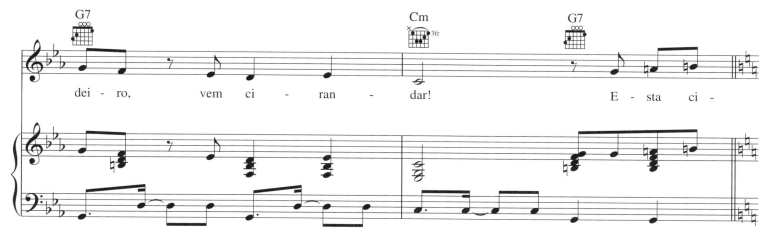

dei - ro, vem ci - ran - dar! E - sta ci -

ran - da quem me deu foi Li - a, que mo - ra na i - lha de I - ta ma - ra - cá!

E - sta ci - ran - da quem me deu foi Li - a, que mo - ra na i -

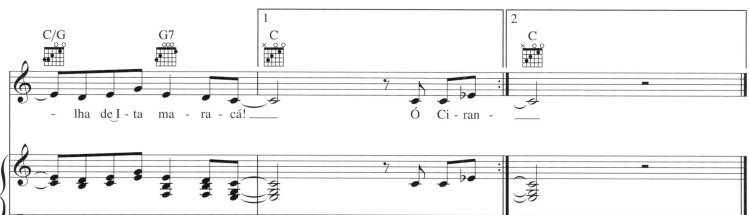

- lha de I - ta ma - ra - cá! Ó Ci - ran -

COCKLES AND MUSSELS
(Molly Malone)

Traditional Irish Folk Song

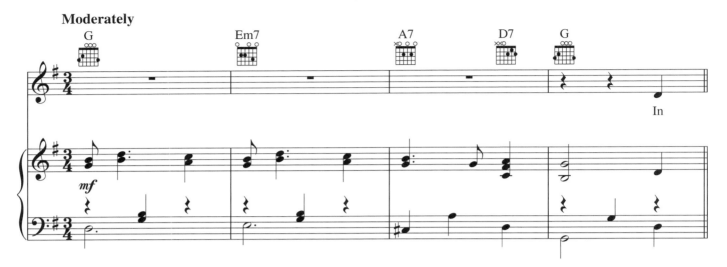

In

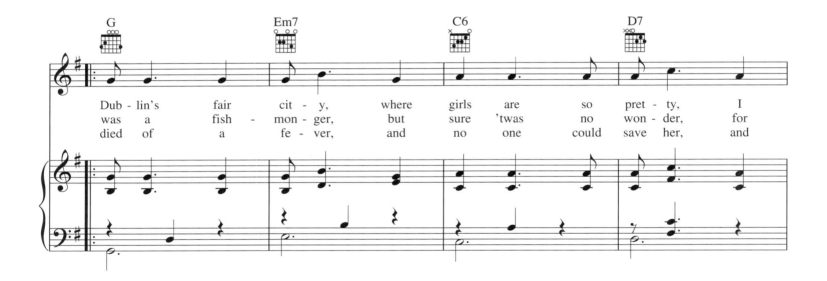

Dub - lin's fair cit - y, where girls are so pret - ty, I
was a fish - mon - ger, but sure 'twas no won - der, for
died of a fe - ver, but and no one could save her, for and

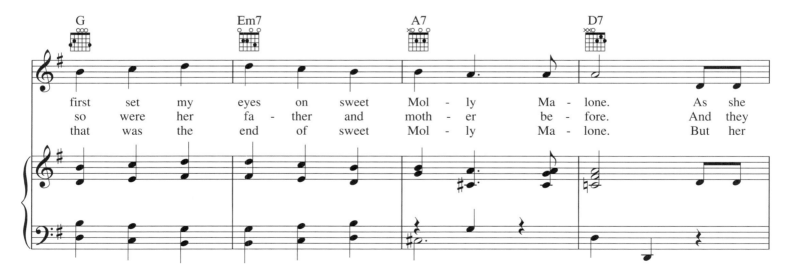

first set my eyes on sweet Mol - ly Ma - lone. As she
so were her fa - ther and moth - er be - fore. And they
that was the end of sweet Mol - ly Ma - lone. But her

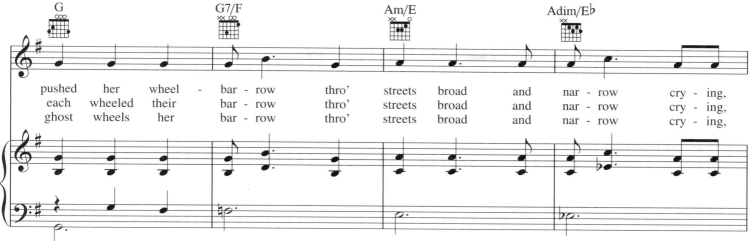

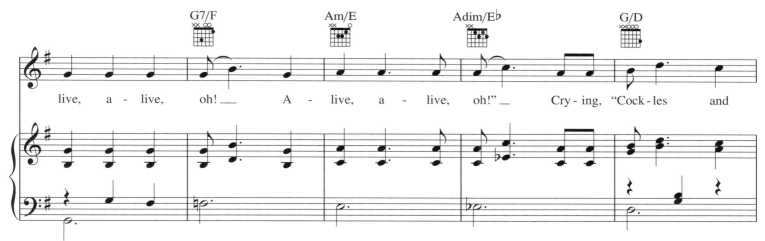

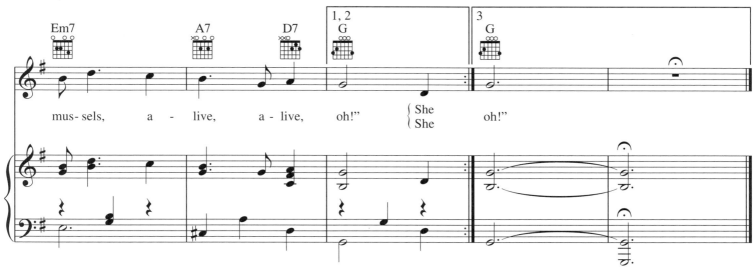

CLAIR DE LUNE

By CLAUDE DEBUSSY

Tempo rubato

pp

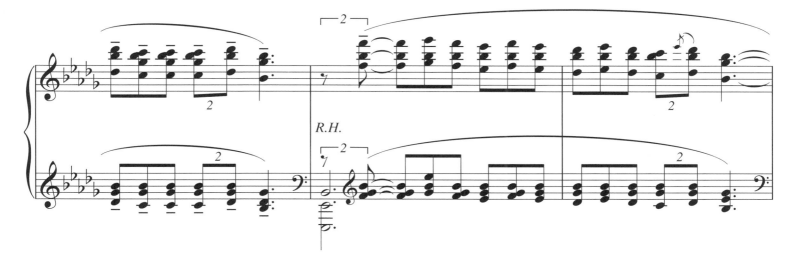

R.H.

peu à peu cresc. et animé (louder and livelier)

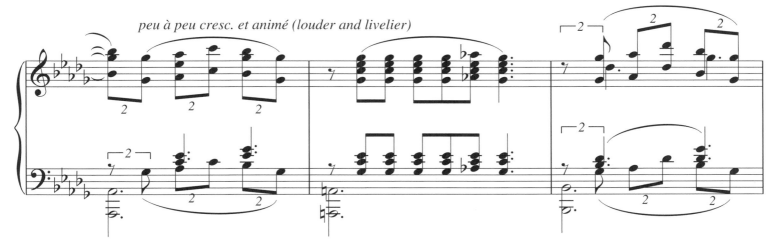

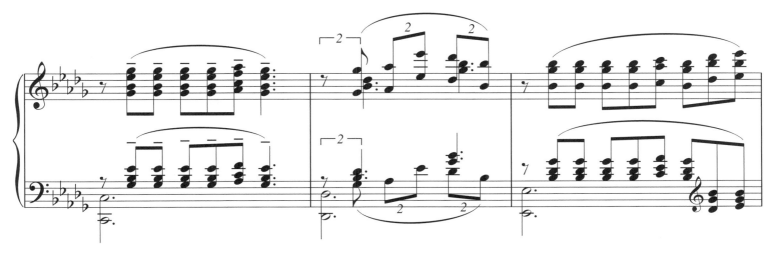

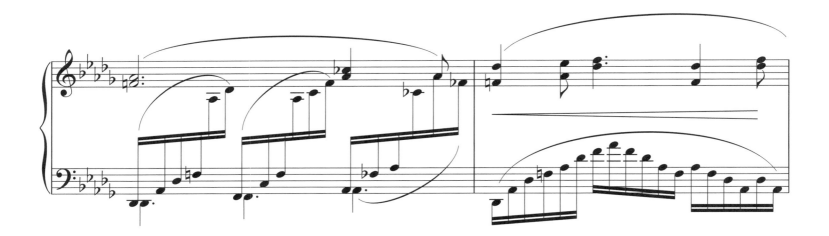

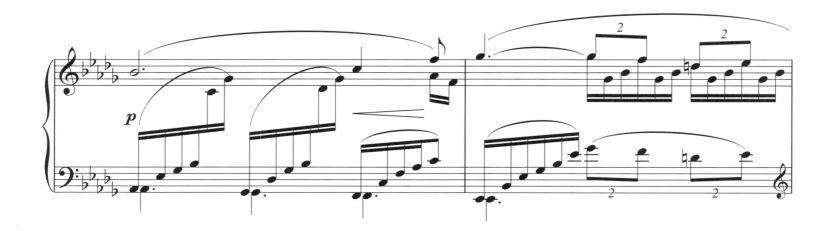

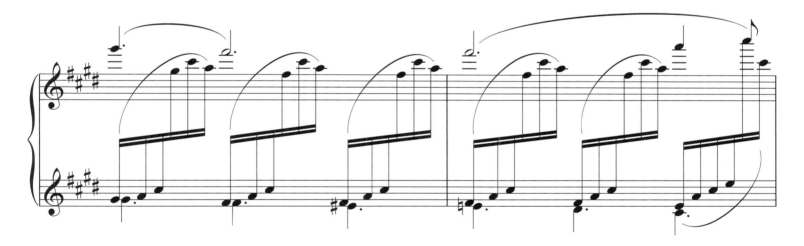

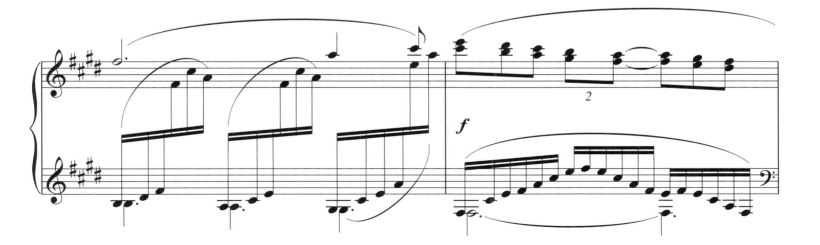

Calmato

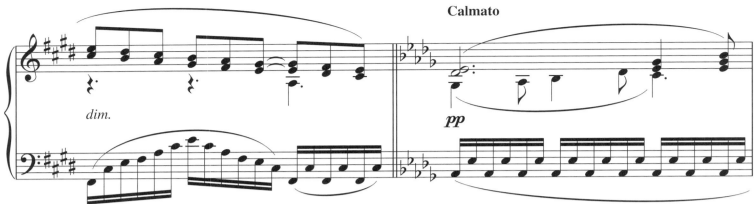

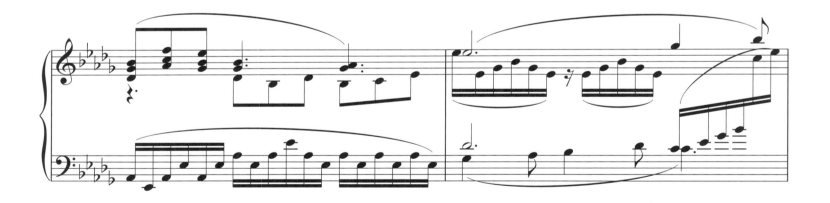

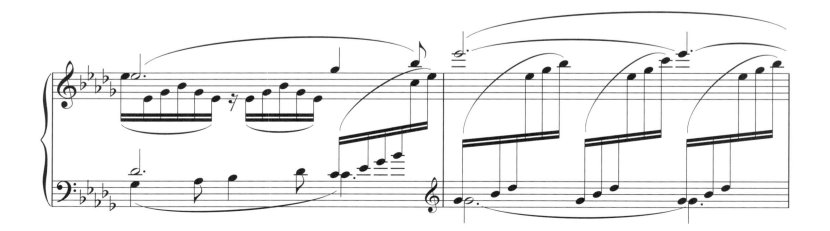

Tempo I

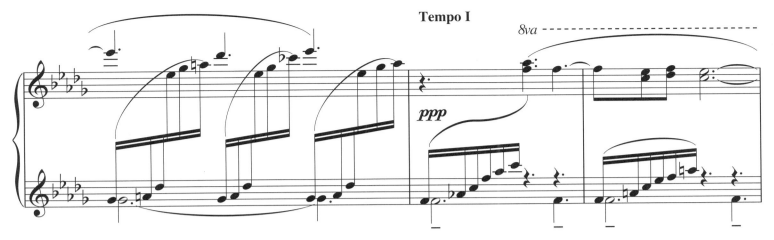

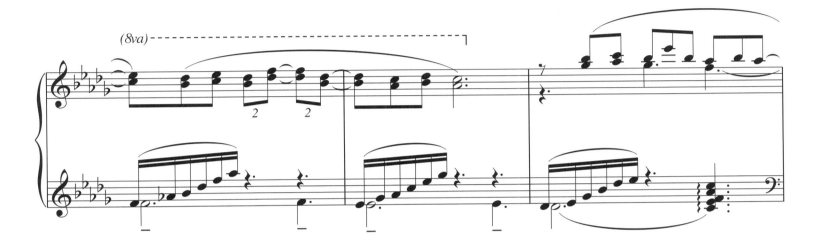

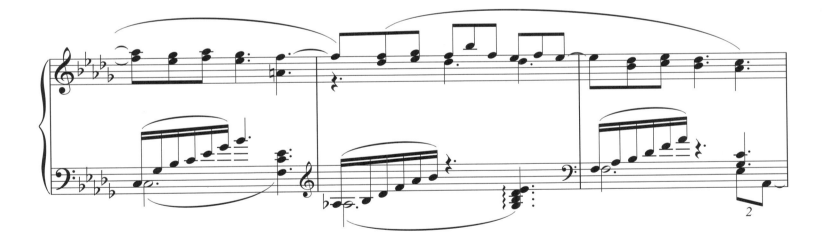

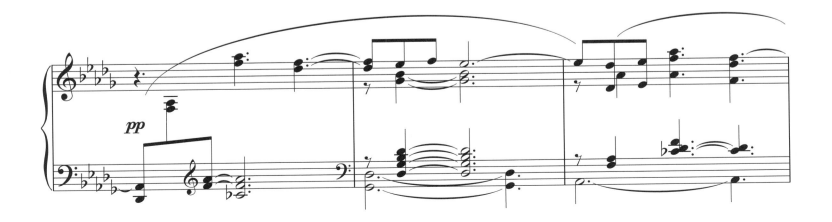

morendo jusqu'à la fin (more and more faint to the end)

DANDANSOY

Traditional Filipino Folk Song

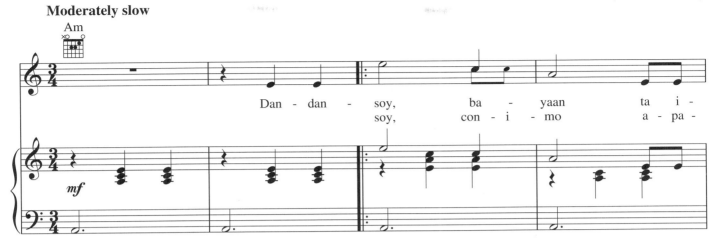

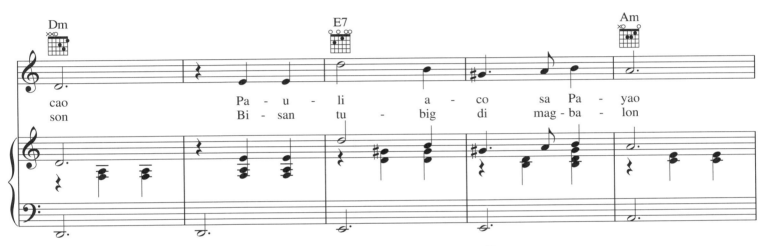

DANNY BOY

Words by FREDERICK EDWARD WEATHERLY
Traditional Irish Folk Melody

back   when sum-mer's in the mead - ow,____ or when the val - ley's hush'd and white with
hear,   though soft your tread a - bove__ me,____ and all my dreams   will warm - er, sweet - er

snow. _____ 'Tis I'll be here   in sun-shine or in shad - ow, ____ oh, Dan - ny
be. _____ Then you will bend   and tell me that you love __ me, _____ and I shall

Boy, oh Dan - ny Boy, I love you so! _____
sleep in peace un - til you come to me! _____

But if ye

DOWN IN THE VALLEY

Traditional American Folk Song

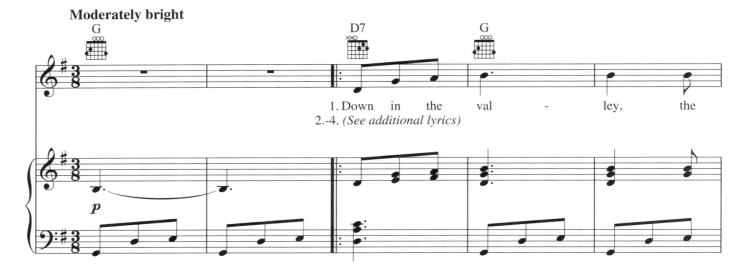

1. Down in the val - ley, the
2.-4. *(See additional lyrics)*

val - ley so low, _____ hang your head o - ver,

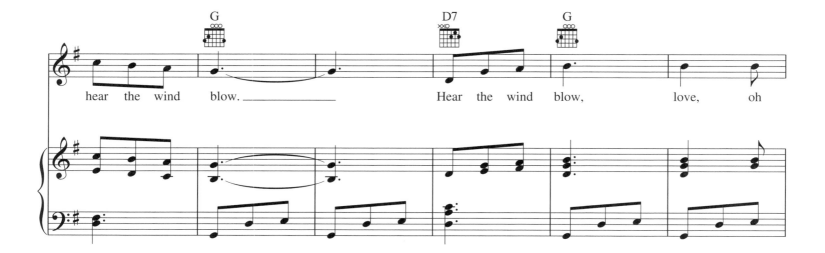

hear the wind blow. _____ Hear the wind blow, love, oh

hear the wind blow, _____ hang your head o - ver,

hear the wind blow. _____

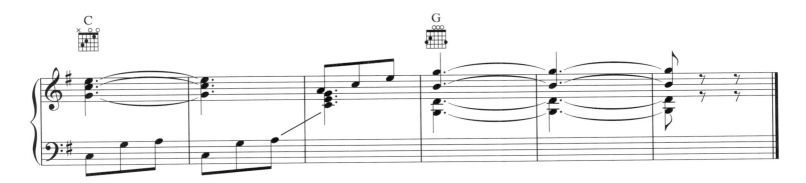

Additional Lyrics

2. Give my heart ease, love, oh give my heart ease,
   Think of me, darling, oh give my heart ease.
   Write me a letter and send it to me,
   Care of the jailhouse in Raleigh, N.C.

3. Write me a letter with just a few lines,
   Answer me, darling, and say you'll be mine.
   Roses love sunshine and violets love dew,
   Angels in Heaven know I love you!

4. This gloomy prison is far from you, dear,
   But not forever; I'm out in a year.
   I make this promise to get straight and true,
   And for a lifetime to love only you!

DRY WEATHER HOUSES

Traditional

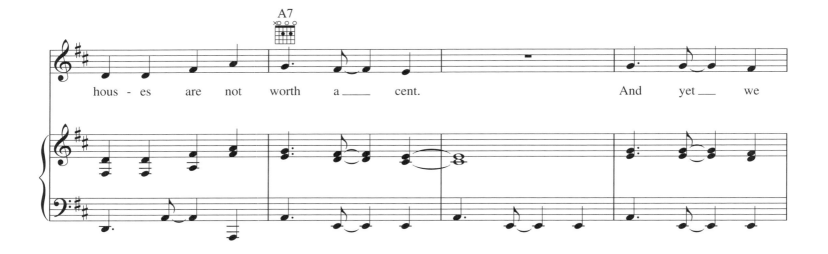

hous - es are not worth a _____ cent. And yet _____ we

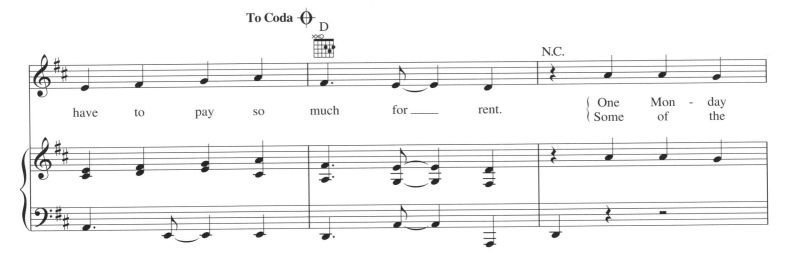

have to pay so much for _____ rent.

{ One Mon - day
{ Some of day the

morn - ing the land - lord went to a ten - ant to get his rent. _____
rooms, they make them so small, you can't turn 'round in them at all. _____

_____ But the ten - ant say, "Mis - ter, me no fool. _____ Me no pay
_____ You go _____ in the yard and cir - cle wide, _____ turn, you're

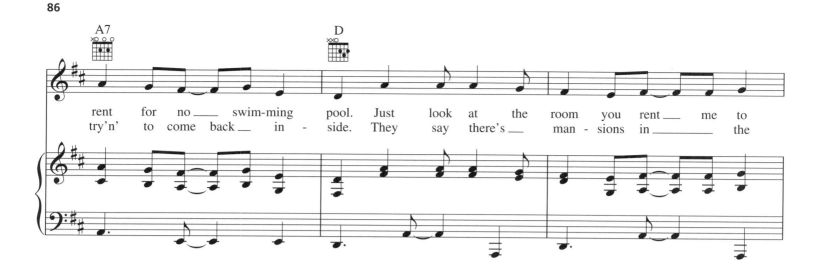

rent for no ___ swim-ming pool. Just look at the room you rent ___ me to
try'n' to come back ___ in - side. They say there's ___ man - sions in _____ the

live. The whole of the roof is just ___ like a sieve. When the rain
sky, ex - pect to go there by ___ and _____ by. Be - fore I

come, if I sleep too sound, ___ so help me, mis - ter, I'll sure - ly
do, I would like a peek ___ just to make cer - tain the roof don't

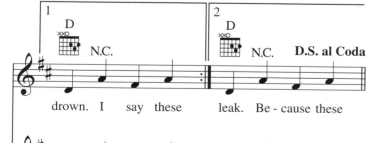

drown. I say these   leak. Be - cause these

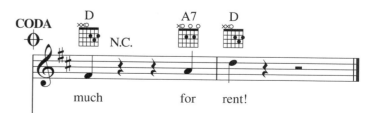

much   for   rent!

DARK EYES

Russian Cabaret Song

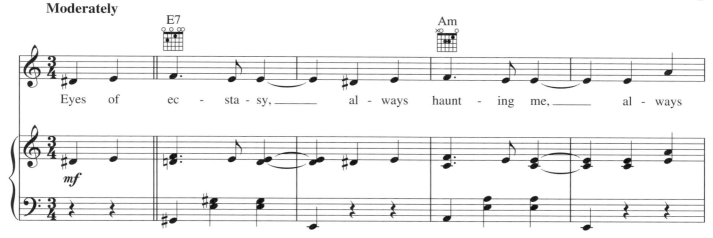

Eyes of ec - sta - sy, _____ al - ways haunt - ing me, _____ al - ways

taunt - ing me _____ with our mus - ter - y! _____ Tell me

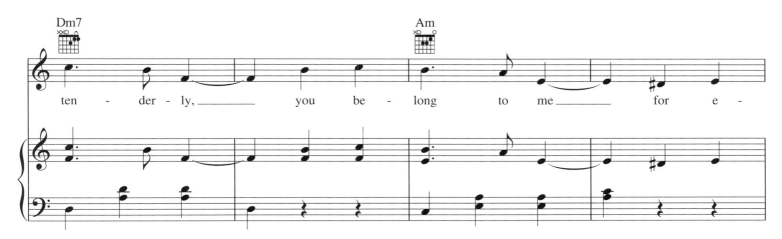

ten - der - ly, _____ you be - long to me _____ for e -

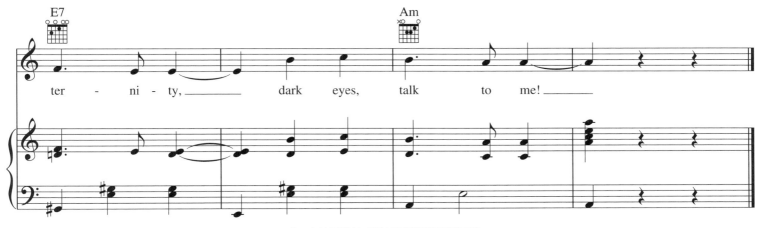

ter - ni - ty, _____ dark eyes, talk to me! _____

DU, DU LIEGST MIR IM HERZEN
(You, You Weigh on My Heart)

German Folk Song

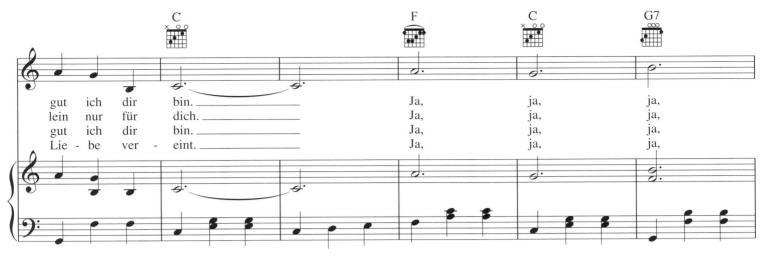

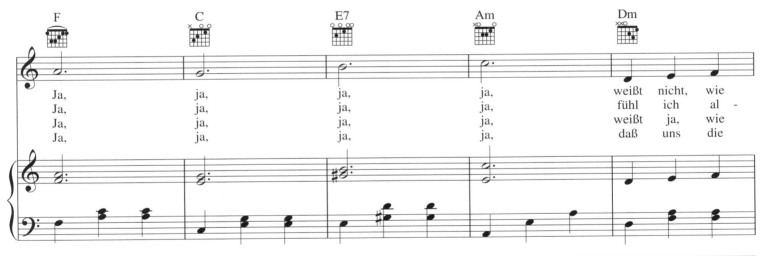

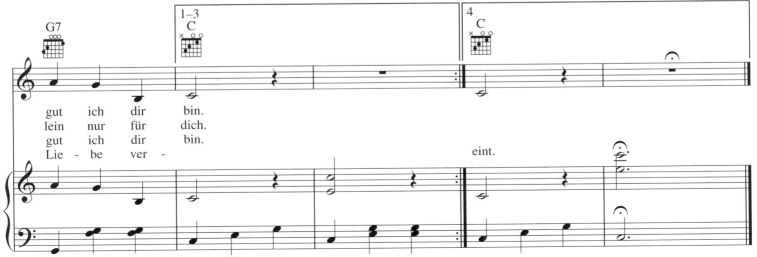

DUERMETE MI NIÑO CHIQUITO
(Go to Sleep, My Little Baby)

Venezuelan Lullaby

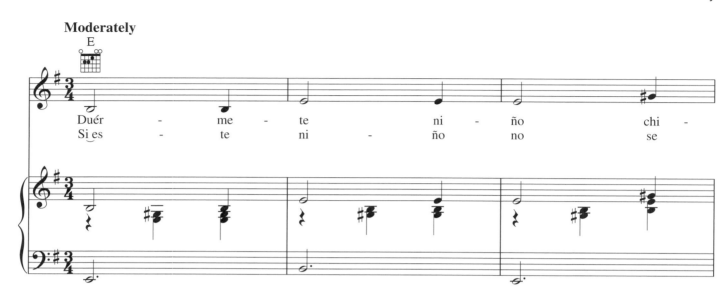

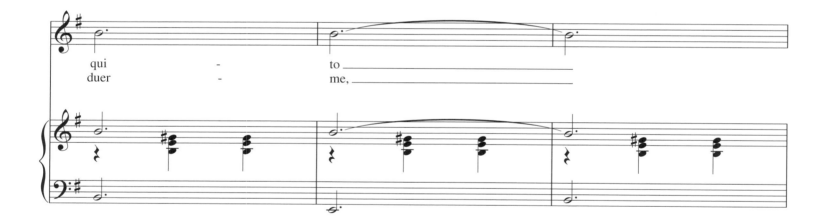

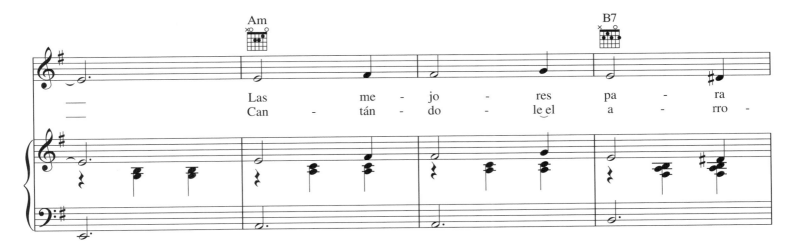

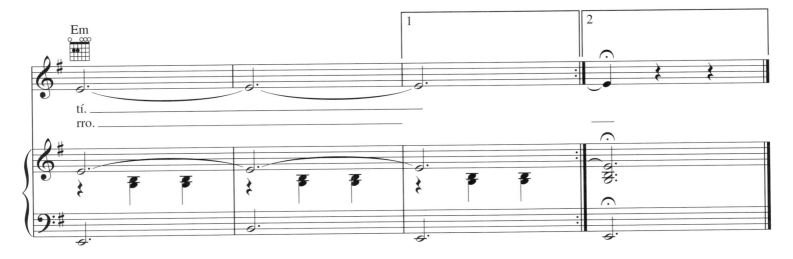

FERRYLAND SEALER

Canadian/Newfoundland Folk Song

1. Oh, our schoon-er and our sloop in Fer-ry-land they do lie. They're al-read-y rigged to be
2. vit-tles for to last more than two months at the least and plen-ty of good rum stowed a-
3.-7. (See additional lyrics)

read-y for the ice. All you lads of the South-ern, we will have you be a-ware she is
way __ in our chest. We will give her a ral-ly for to praise __ all our fan-cy. All our

Additional Lyrics

3. Our course be east-north-east two days and two nights,
   Our captain he cried out, "Boys, look ahead for the ice!"
   And we hove her about standing in for the land,
   And 'twas in a few hours we were firm in the jam.

4. Oh, our captain he cried out, "Come on, boys, and bear a'hand."
   Our cook he gets the breakfast and each man takes a dram,
   With their bats in their hands it was earlye to go,
   Every man showed his action 'thout the missing of a blow.

5. Some were killing, some were scalping, some were hauling on board
   And some more they were firing and a-missing of their loads.
   In the dusk of the evening all hands in from the cold,
   And we counted nine hundred fine scalps in the hold.

6. Oh, now we are loaded and our schooner she is sound,
   And the ice it is open and to Ferryland we're bound,
   We all gave her a rally for to praise all our fancy,
   Our seals they were collected by the William and the Nancy.

7. We are now off Cape Spear and in sight of Cape Broyle,
   We will dance, sing, carouse, my boys, in just a little while,
   We will soon enjoy the charms of our sweethearts and friends
   For it will not be long before we're down to the bend.

FINNEGAN'S WAKE

Traditional Irish Folk Song

Moderately

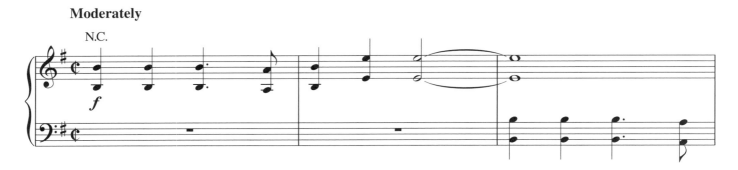

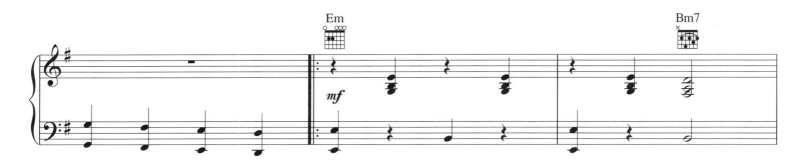

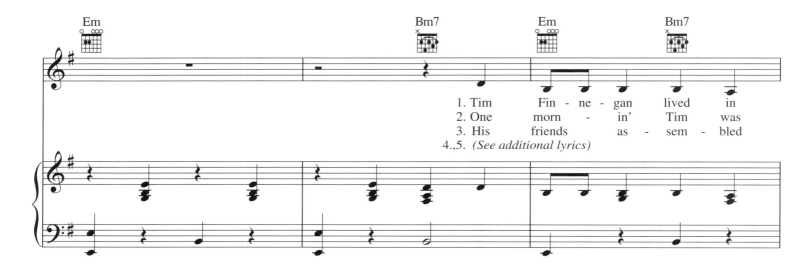

1. Tim Fin - ne - gan lived in
2. One morn - in' Tim was
3. His friends as - sem - bled
4., 5. *(See additional lyrics)*

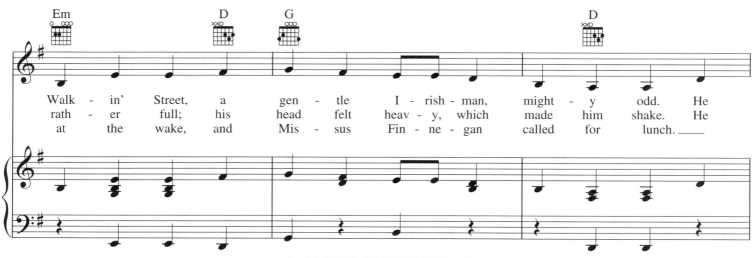

Walk - in' Street, a gen - tle I - rish - man, might - y odd. He
rath - er full; his head felt heav - y, which made him shake. He
at the wake, and Mis - sus Fin - ne - gan called for lunch. ___

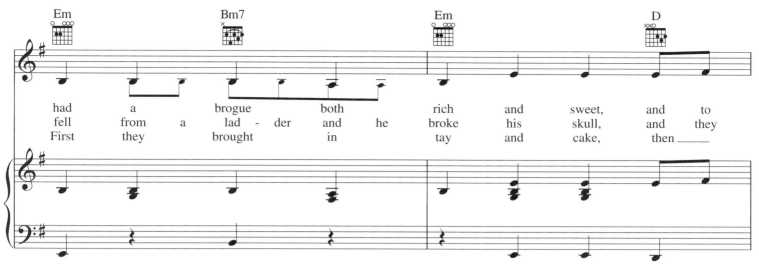

had a brogue both rich and sweet, and to
fell from a lad - der and he broke his skull, and they
First they brought in tay and cake, then _____

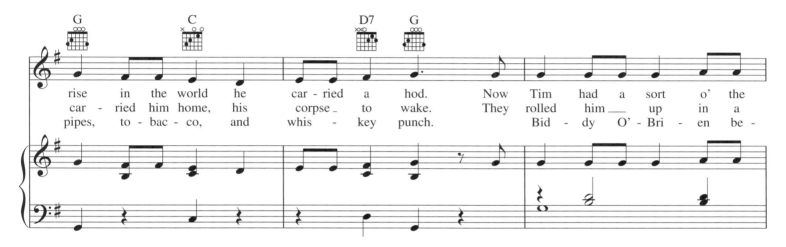

rise in the world he car - ried a hod. Now Tim had a sort o' the
car - ried him home, his corpse to wake. They rolled him _____ up in a
pipes, to - bac - co, and whis - key punch. Bid - dy O' - Bri - en be -

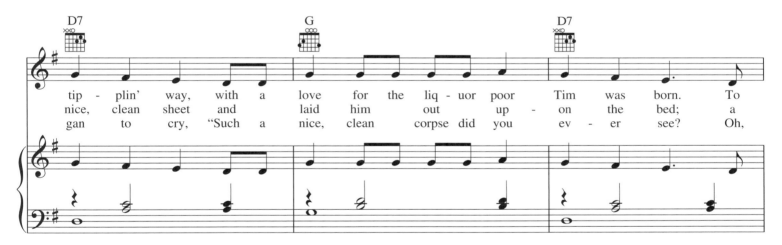

tip - plin' way, with a love for the liq - uor poor Tim was born. To
nice, clean sheet and laid him out up - on the bed; a
gan to cry, "Such a nice, clean corpse did you ev - er see? Oh,

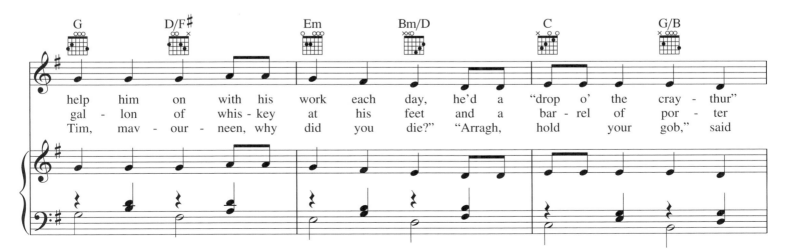

help him on with his work each day, he'd a "drop o' the cray - thur"
gal - lon of whis - key at his feet and a bar - rel of por - ter
Tim, mav - our - neen, why did you die?" "Arragh, hold your gob," said

Chorus

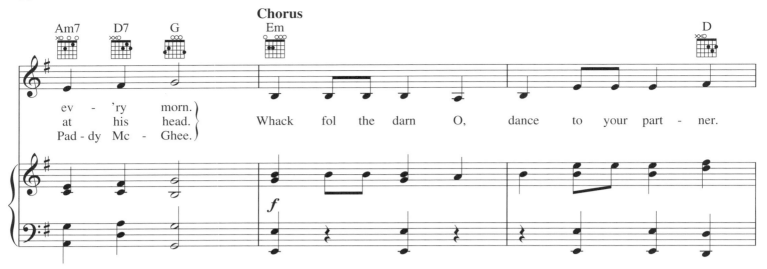

ev - 'ry morn.
at his head.
Pad - dy Mc - Ghee.

Whack fol the darn O, dance to your part - ner.

Whirl the floor, your trot - ters shake; was - n't it the

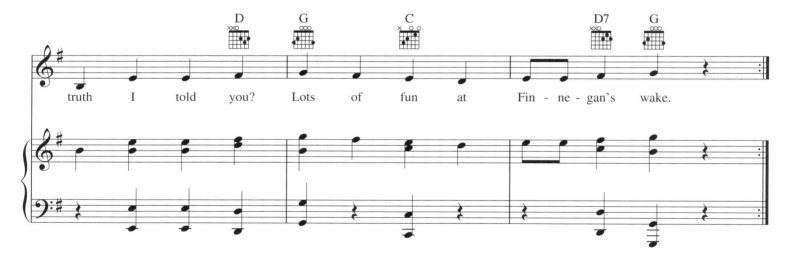

truth I told you? Lots of fun at Fin - ne - gan's wake.

Additional Lyrics

4. Then Maggie O'Connor took up the job,
   "Oh Biddy," says she, "you're wrong, I'm sure."
   Biddy, she gave her a belt in the gob
   And left her sprawlin' on the floor.
   And then the war did soon engage,
   'Twas woman to woman and man to man.
   Shillelaigh law was all the rage,
   And a row and ruction soon began.
   Chorus

5. Then Mickey Maloney ducked his head
   When a noggin of whiskey flew at him.
   It missed, and falling on the bed,
   The liquor scattered over Tim!
   The corpse revives; see how he rises!
   Timothy, rising from the bed,
   Said, "Whirl your whiskey around like blazes,
   Thanum an Dhul! Do you think I'm dead?"
   Chorus

DUERME NIÑO PEQUEÑITO
(Sleep, My Baby, Precious Darling)

Colombian Folk Song

FLOWERS OF JOY

Swedish Folk Song

Gläd - jens blom - ster i jor - dens mull, ack, visst al - drig gro. Kär - lek själv ju för - såt - lig är för ditt hjär - tas ro.

Men där ov - an, för hopp ach tro, blom - stra de e - vigt

fris - ka. Hör du ei hur an - dar ljuvt om dem till hjär - tat

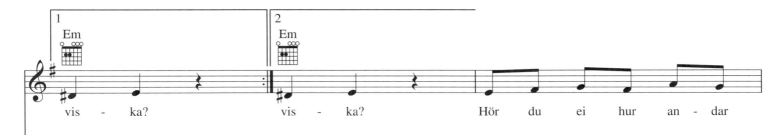

vis - ka? | vis - ka? Hör du ei hur an - dar

ljuvt om dem till hjär - tat vis - ka?

FUNICULI, FUNICULA

Words and Music by
LUIGI DENZA

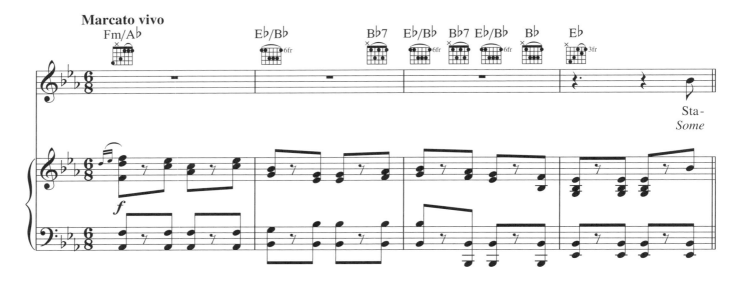

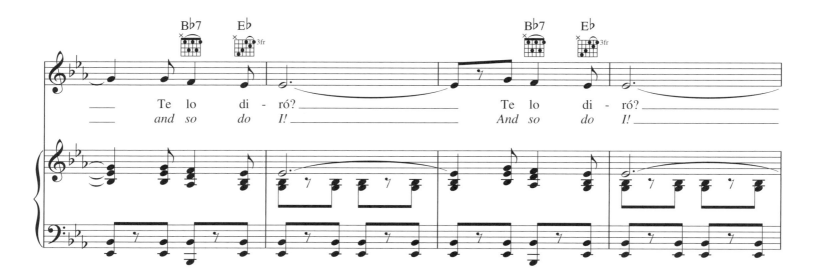

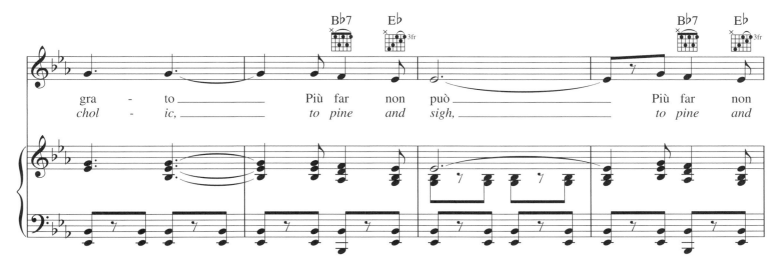

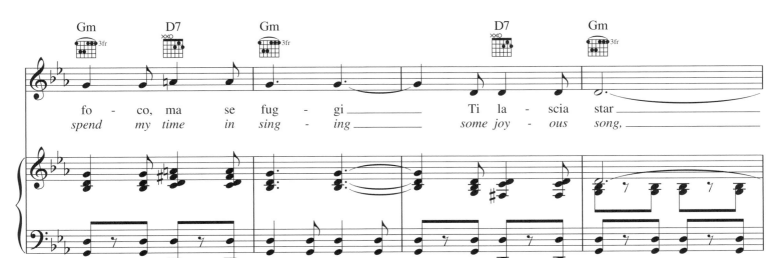

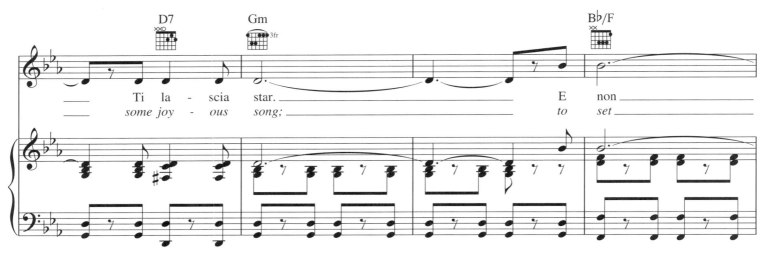

Ti la - scia star. _____ E non _____
some joy - ous song; _____ to set _____

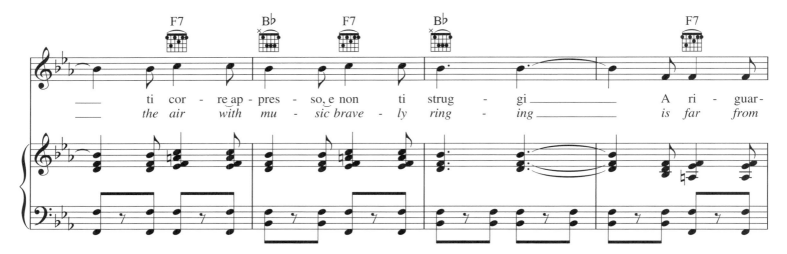

ti cor - re ap - pres - so, e non ti strug - gi _____ A ri - guar
the air with mu - sic brave - ly ring - ing _____ is far from

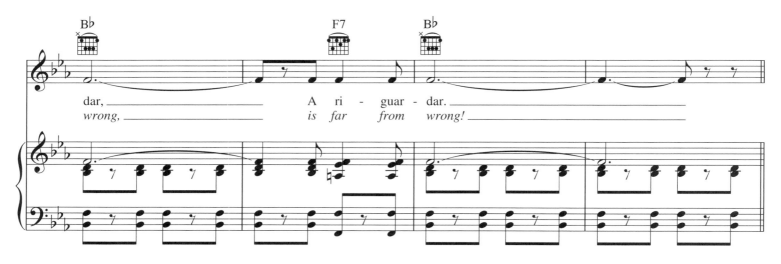

dar, _____ A ri - guar - dar. _____
wrong, _____ is far from wrong! _____

Le - sti, le - sti, via mon - tiam su là _____
Lis - ten, lis - ten, ech - oes sound a - far! _____

le - sti, le - sti, via mon-tiam su là fu - ni - cu -
Lis - ten, lis - ten, ech - oes sound a - far fu - ni - cu -

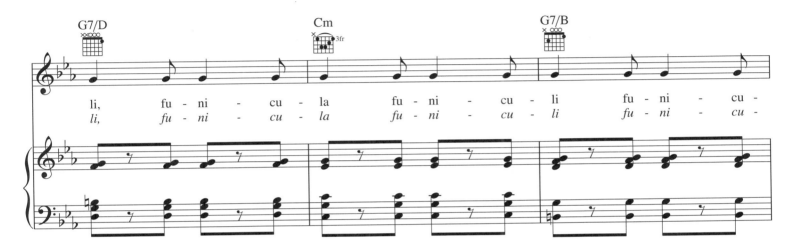

li, fu - ni - cu - la fu - ni - cu - li fu - ni - cu -
li, fu - ni - cu - la fu - ni - cu - li fu - ni - cu -

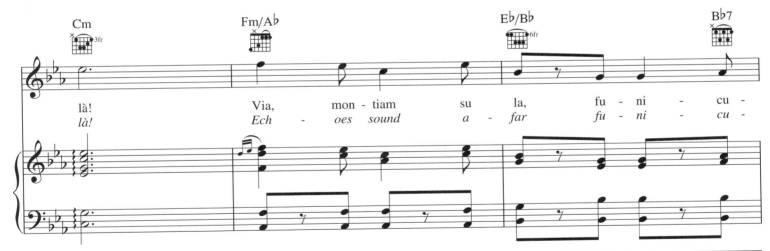

là! Via, mon - tiam su la, fu - ni - cu -
là! Ech - oes sound a - far fu - ni - cu -

li fu - ni - cu - là. li fu - ni - cu - là. _____
li fu - ni - cu - là. li fu - ni - cu - là. _____

GABI, GABI

South African Praise Song

Ga - bi, Ga - bi, ___

Ga - bi, Ga - bi, ___   Ga - bi, Ga - bi, ___   Ga - bi, Ga - bi, ___

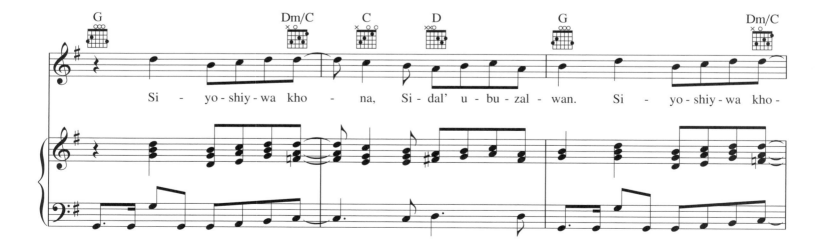

Si - yo - shiy - wa kho - na, Si - dal' u - bu - zal - wan. Si - yo - shiy - wa kho -

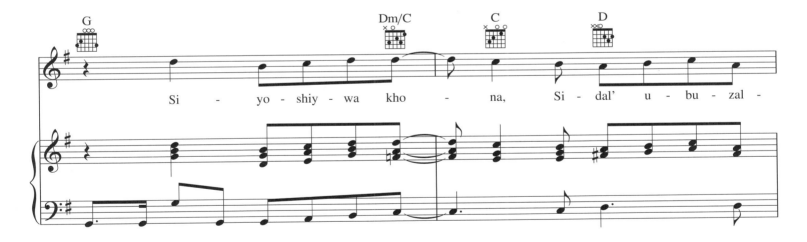

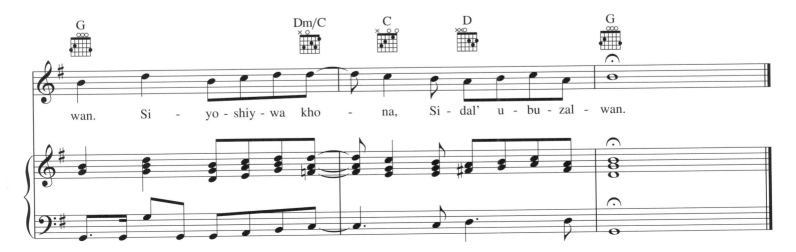

GREENSLEEVES

16th Century Traditional English

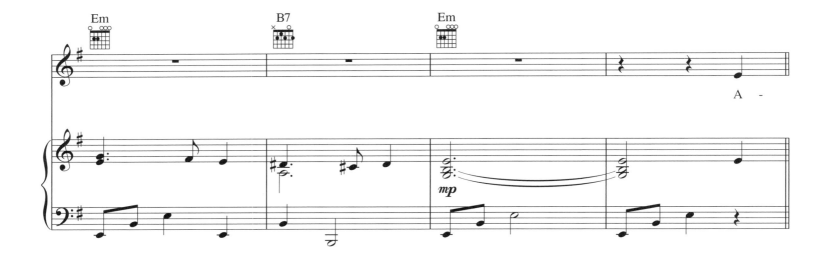

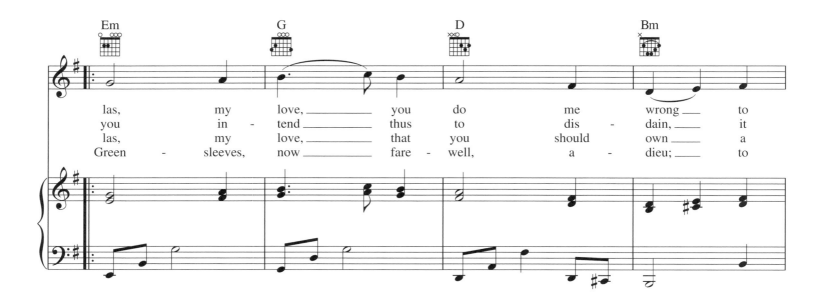

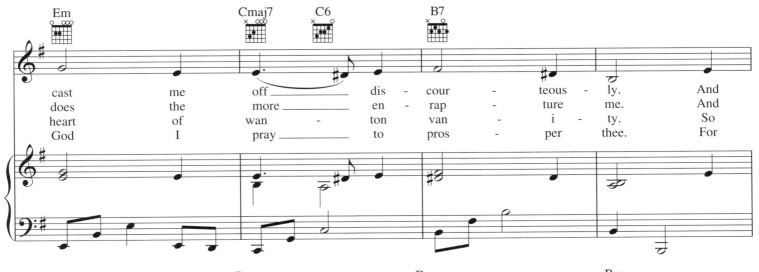

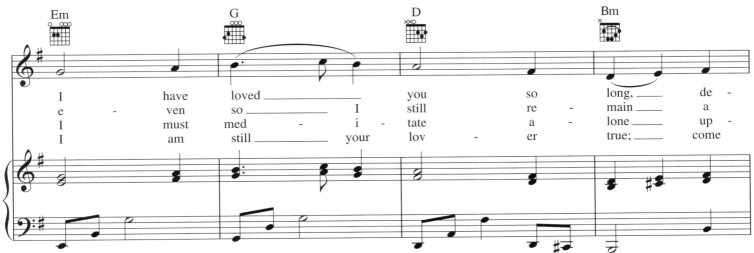

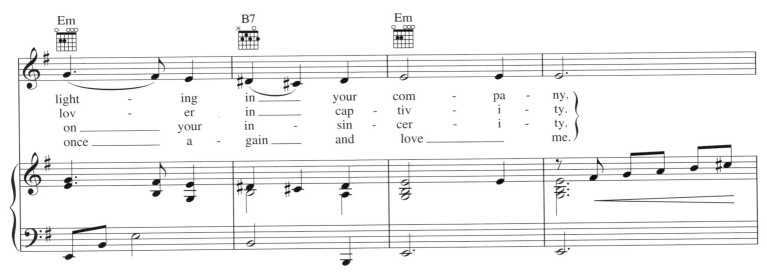

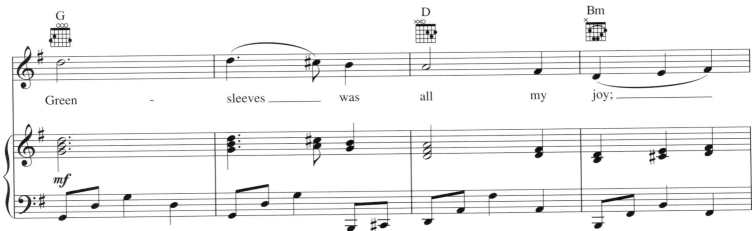

Green - sleeves _____ was my de -

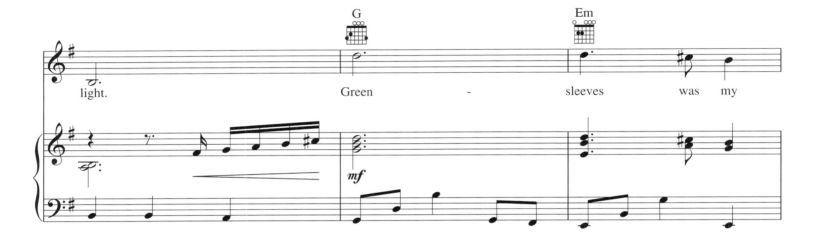

light. Green - sleeves was my

heart of gold, _____ and who but my la - dy

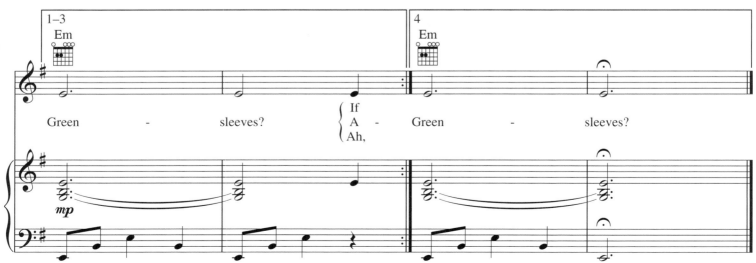

Green - sleeves?

If
A - Green - sleeves?
Ah,

FRÈRE JACQUES
(Are You Sleeping?)

Traditional

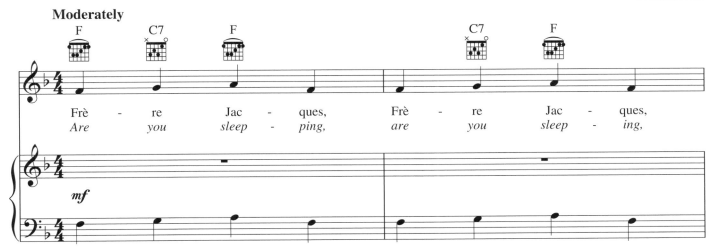

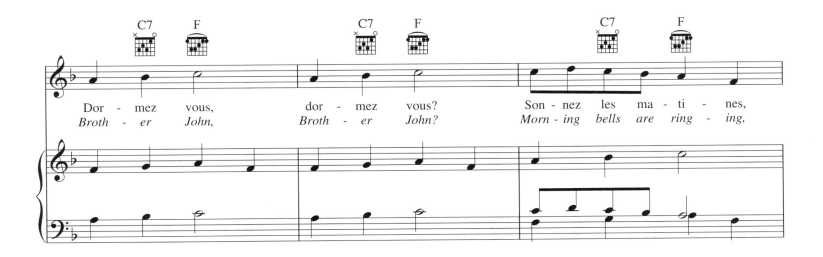

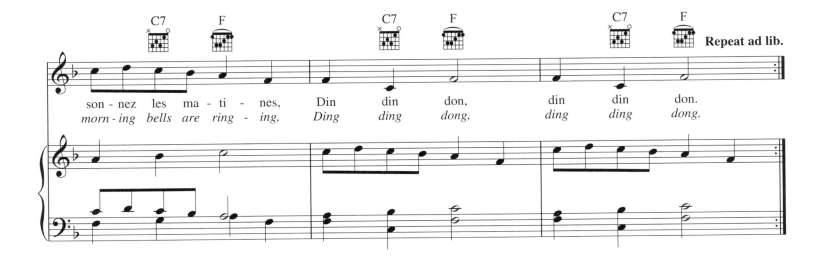

GUANTANAMERA

Cuban Folk Song

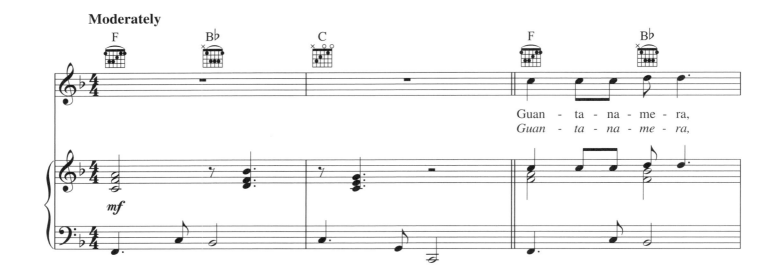

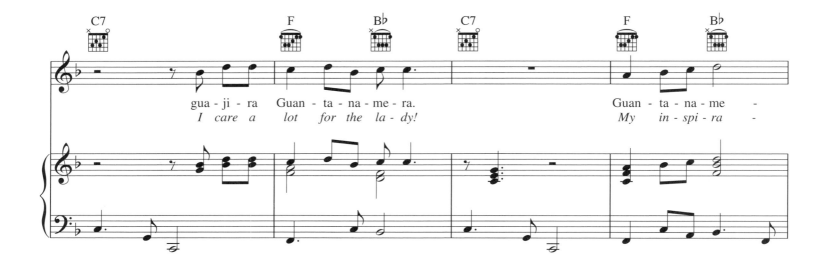

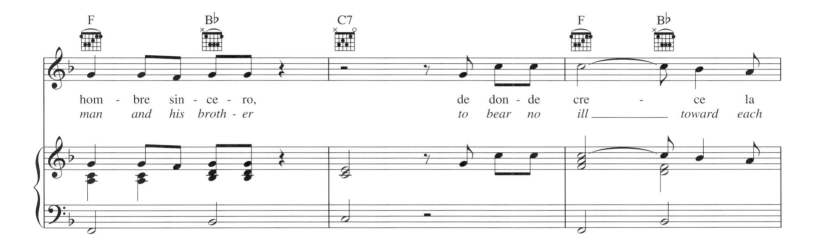

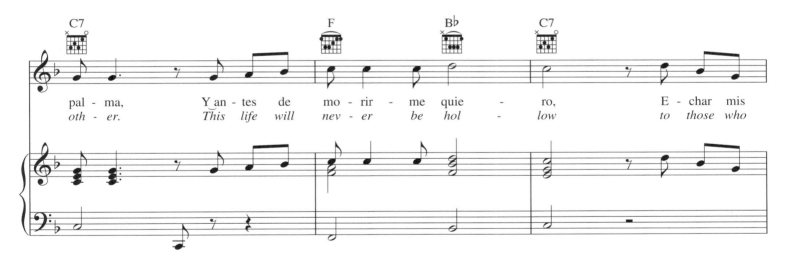

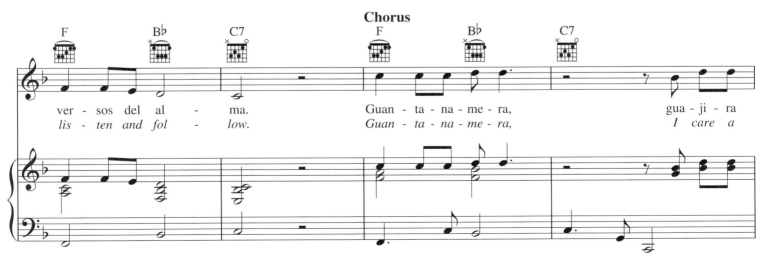

Additional Spanish Lyrics

2. Mi verso es de un verde claro,
   Y de un carmin encendido,
   Mi verso es un ciervo herido,
   Que busca en el monte amparo.
   Chorus

3. Con los pobres de la tierra,
   Quiero yo mi suerte echar,
   El arroyo de la sierra,
   Me complace mas que el mar.
   Chorus

Additional English Lyrics

2. *I write my rhymes with no learning,*
   And yet with truth they are burning,
   But is the world waiting for them?
   Or will they all just ignore them?
   Have I a poet's illusion,
   A dream to die in seclusion?
   Chorus

3. *A little brook on a mountain,*
   The cooling spray of a fountain
   Arouse in me an emotion,
   More than the vast boundless ocean,
   For there's a wealth beyond measure
   In little things that we treasure.
   Chorus (in Spanish)

HATIKVAH
(With Hope)

Traditional Hebrew Melody
Lyrics by N.H. IMBER

Andante espressivo ($\quad$ = 76)

With pedal

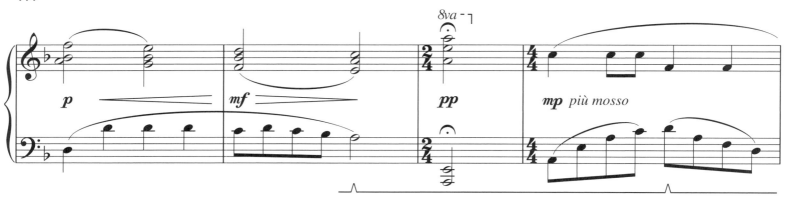

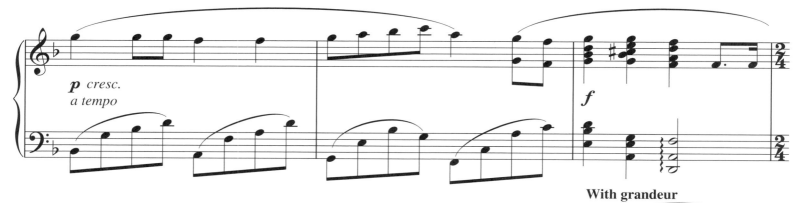

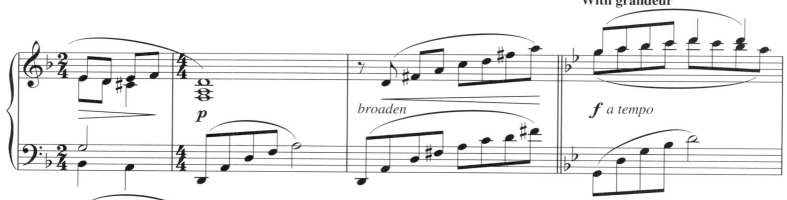

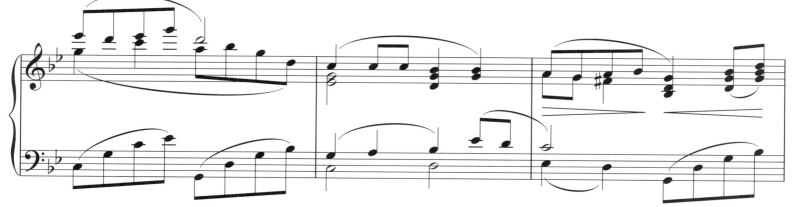

HAVA NAGILA
(Let's Be Happy)

Lyrics by MOSHE NATHANSON
Music by ABRAHAM Z. IDELSOHN

With spirit

Ha - va nagila hava nagila

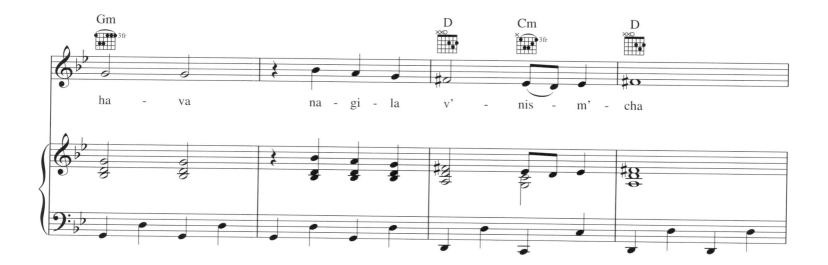

ha - va nagila v'- nis - m'- cha

ha - va nagila hava nagila hava

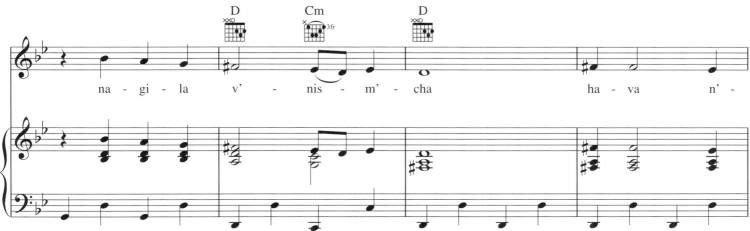

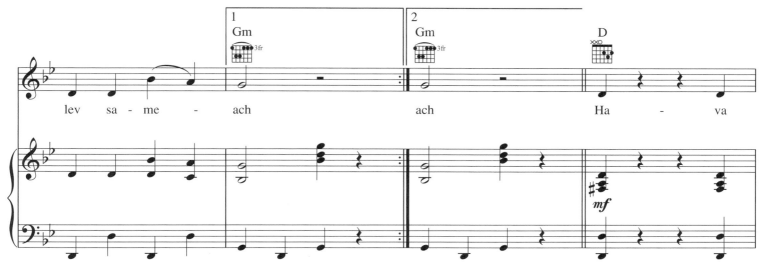

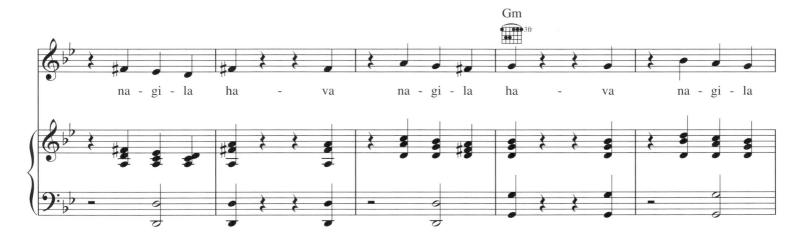

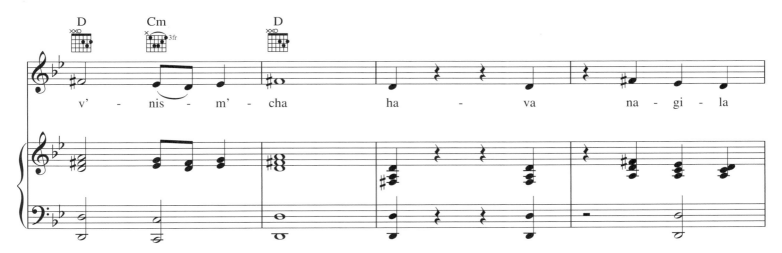

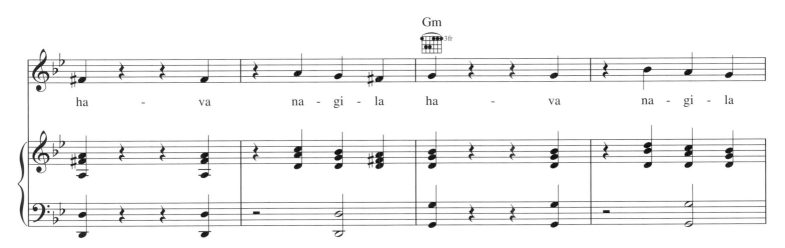

v' - nis - m' - cha ha - va n' - ra - n' - na ha - va n' -

ra - n' - na ha - va n' - ra - n' - na v' - nis - m' -

cha ha - va n' - ra - n' - na ha - va n' - ra - n' - na

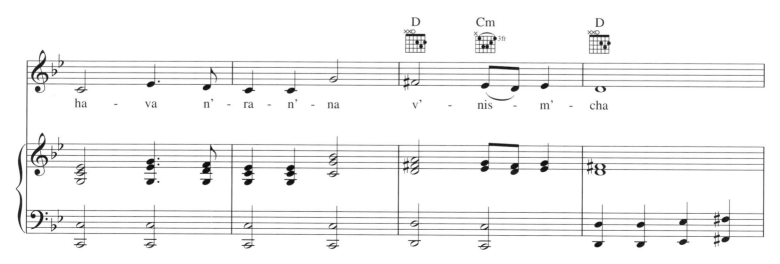

ha - va n' - ra - n' - na v' - nis - m' - cha

THE HURON CAROL

Traditional French-Canadian Text
Traditional Canadian-Indian Melody

fore the light the stars grew dim, and won - d'ring hunt - ers
as the hunt - er braves drew nigh, and the an - gel song rang
chiefs from far be - fore Him knelt with gifts of fur and
kneel be - fore the ra - diant Boy who brings you beau - ty,

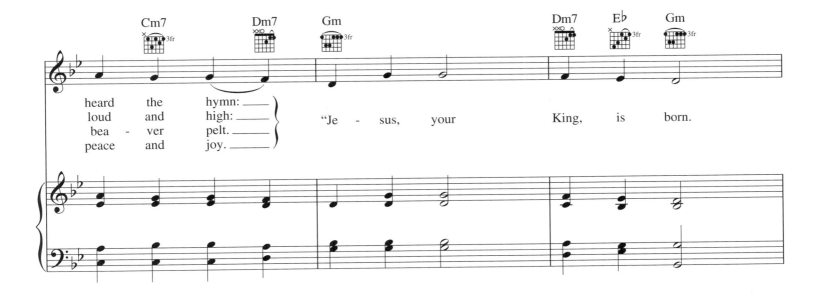

heard the hymn: _____ ⎫
loud and high: _____ ⎬ "Je - sus, your King, is born.
bea - ver pelt. _____ ⎪
peace and joy. _____ ⎭

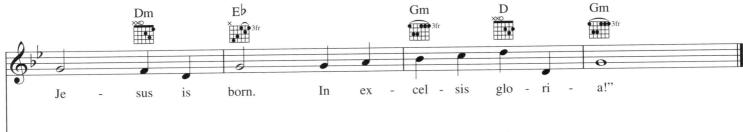

Je - sus is born. In ex - cel - sis glo - ri - a!"

I'S THE B'Y

Traditional Newfoundland Folk Song

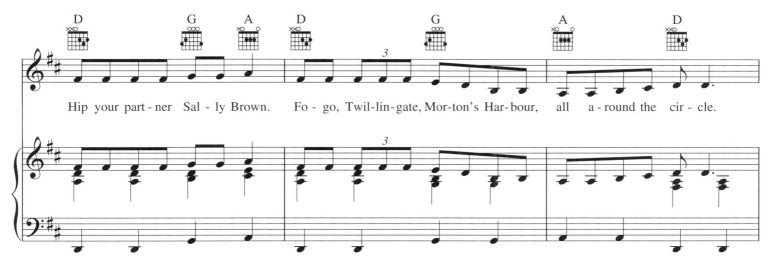

Hip your part-ner Sal-ly Brown. Fo-go, Twil-lin-gate, Mor-ton's Har-bour, all a-round the cir-cle.

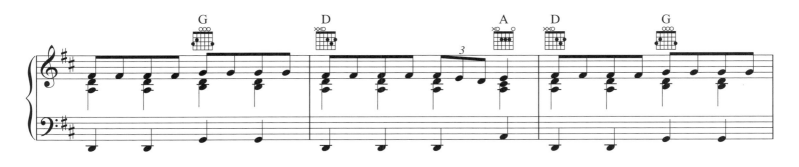

Well, I took Liz-er to a dance and faith, but she could trav-el! And
Now Su-san White, she's out of sight, her pet-ti-coat wants a bor-der. And

ev-'ry step that she did take was up to her knees in grav-el.
old Sir Ol-i-ver in the dark he kissed her in the cor-ner.

I'VE BEEN WORKING ON THE RAILROAD

American Folk Song

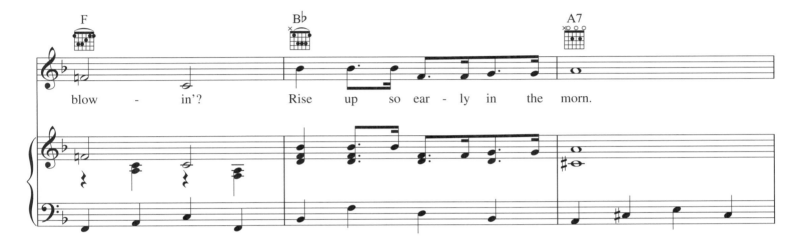

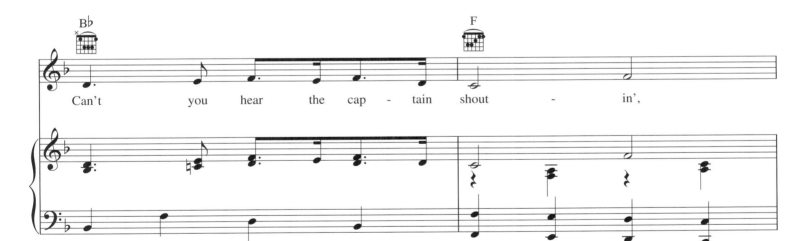

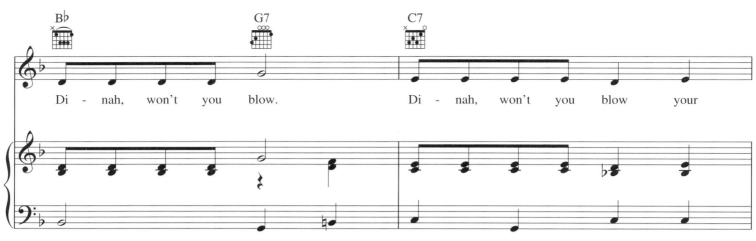

Di - nah, won't you blow. Di - nah, won't you blow your

horn? _____ Di - nah, won't you blow, Di - nah, won't you blow,

Di - nah, won't you blow your horn? Some-one's in the kitch - en with

Di - nah. Some-one's in the kitch - en I know. _____

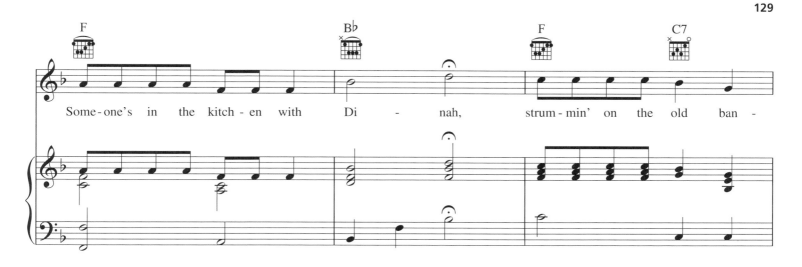

Some-one's in the kitch-en with Di - nah, strum-min' on the old ban -

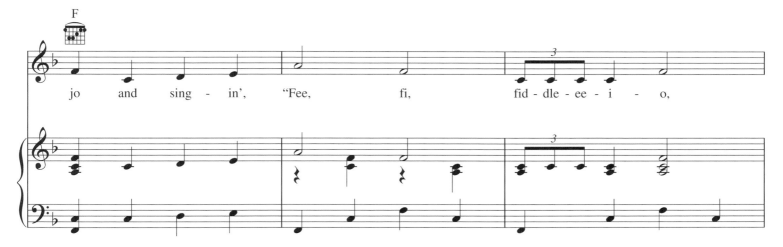

jo and sing - in', "Fee, fi, fid - dle - ee - i - o,

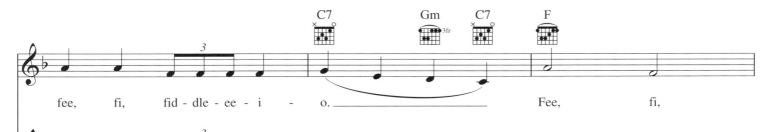

fee, fi, fid - dle - ee - i - o. _____ Fee, fi,

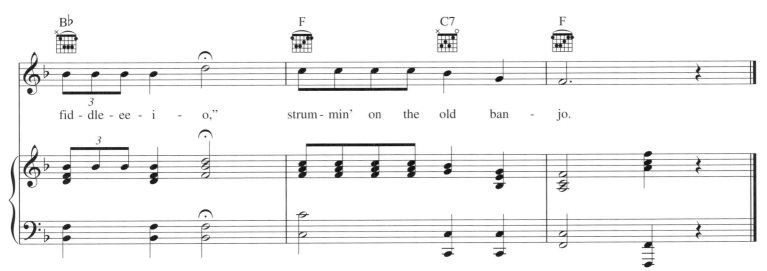

fid - dle - ee - i - o," strum-min' on the old ban - jo.

IL BACIO
(The Kiss)

By LUIGI ARDITI

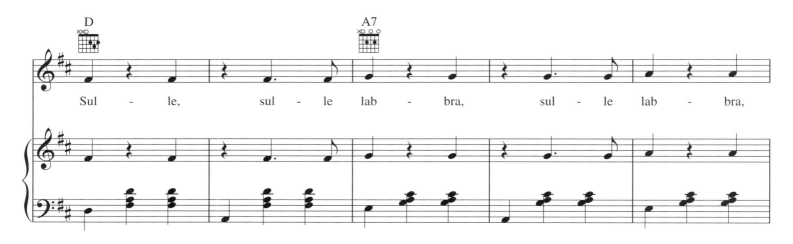

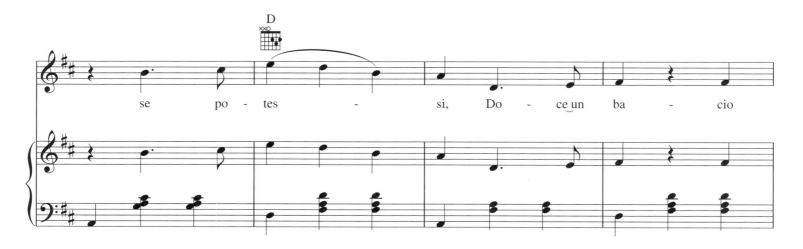

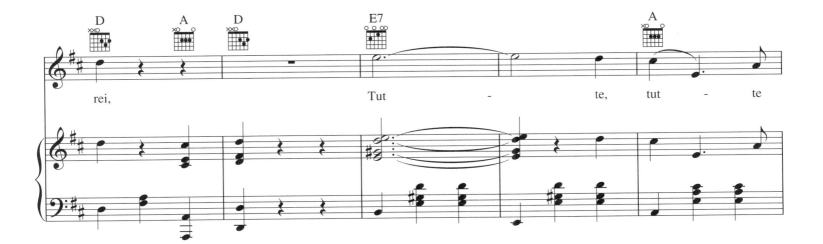

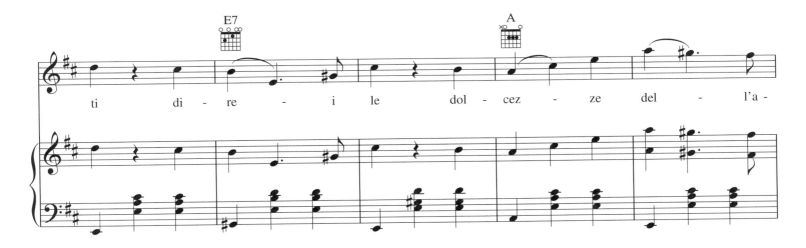

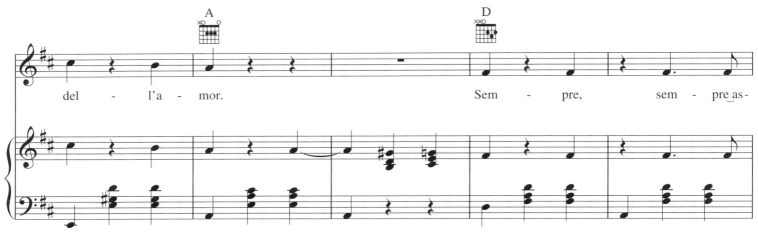

del - l'a - mor. Sem - pre, sem - pre as -

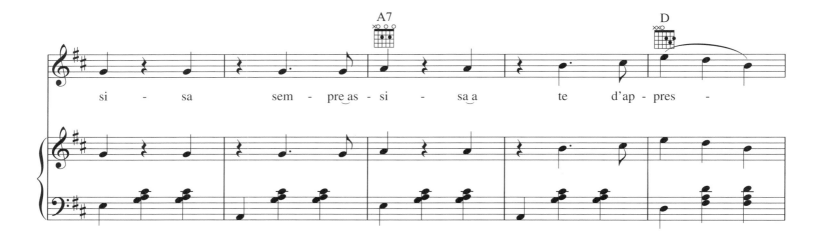

si - sa sem - pre as - si - sa a te d'ap - pres -

so, Mil - le re - i - ti di - re _____ i, mil - le

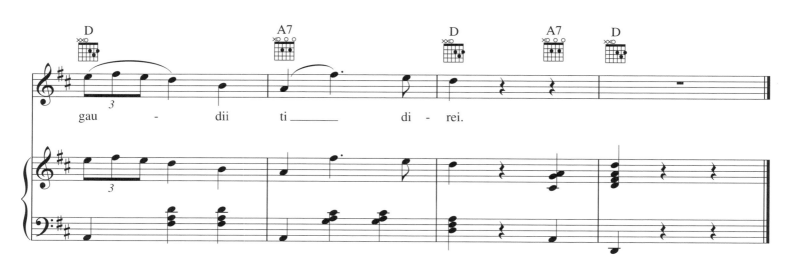

gau - dii ti _____ di - rei.

HOE LAAT IS'T?
(What Time Is It?)

Netherlands Folk Song

IMPUKU NEKATI
(The Mouse and Cat)

African Folk Song

im-pu-ku ne-ka-ti zi-ya-wa ny-a-wu zi-thi ny-a-wu zi-thi zi-thi ne-ka-ti

ny-a-wu zi-thi ny-a-wu zi-thi ny. Im-pu-ku ne-ka-ti zi-ya-wa-le-qu-na

im-pu-ku ne-ka-ti zi-ya-wa ny-a-wu zi-thi ny-a-wu zi-thi

zi-thi ne-ka-ti ny-a-wu zi-thi ny-a-wu zi-thi ny.

ITALIAN STREET SONG

Lyrics by RIDA JOHNSON YOUNG
Music by VICTOR HERBERT

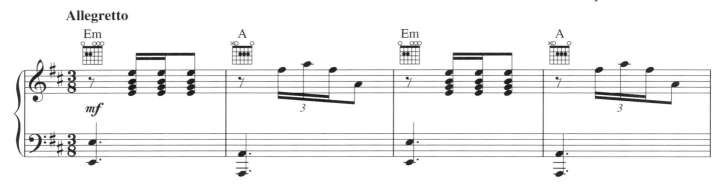

seem to hear a - gain in dreams _____ her

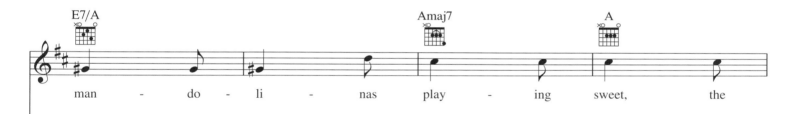

rev - el - ry, _____ her sweet rev - el - ry. _____ The

man - do - li - nas play - ing sweet, the

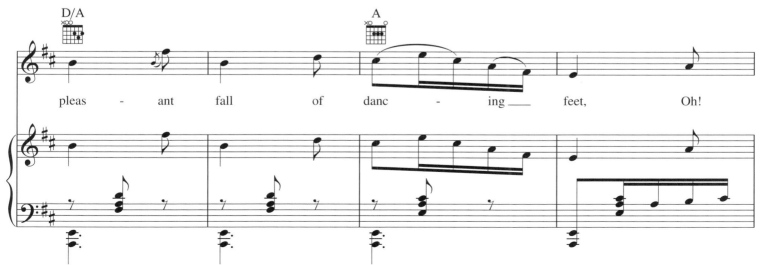

pleas - ant fall of danc - ing ___ feet, Oh!

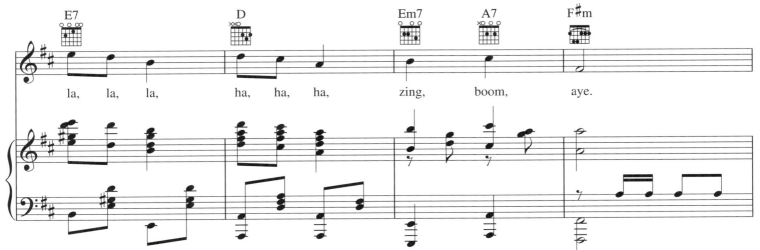

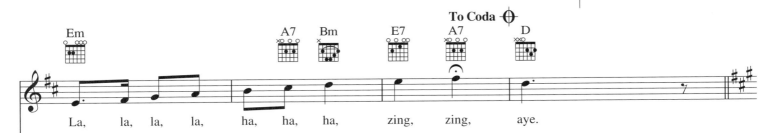

la,

la, la, la, la, zing!

La, la, la, la!

Ziz-zy, ziz-zy, zing, zing, zing, ziz-zy, ziz-zy, zing, zing,

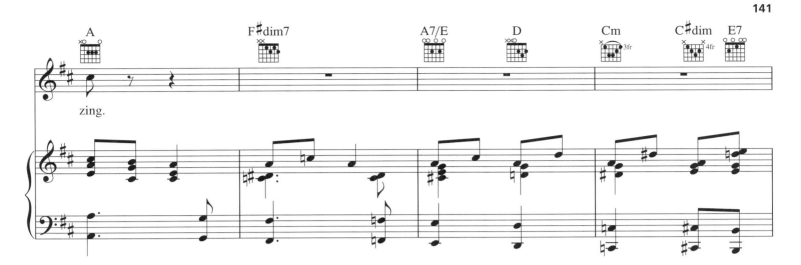

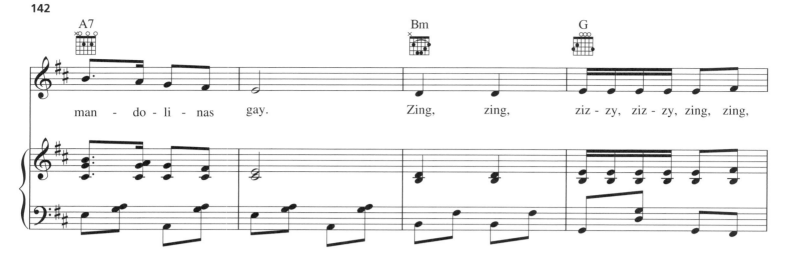

man - do - li - nas gay. Zing, zing, ziz - zy, ziz - zy, zing, zing,

boom, ___ boom, ___ aye, la, la, la,

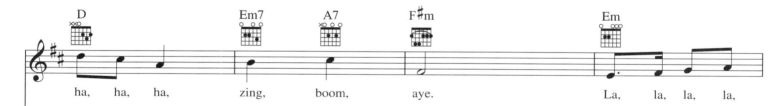

ha, ha, ha, zing, boom, aye. La, la, la, la,

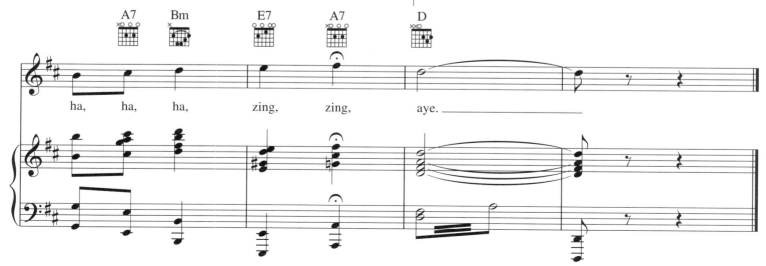

ha, ha, ha, zing, zing, aye. _____

IROQUOIS LULLABY

Canadian Folk Song

Moderately slow

Ho, ho, ___ Wa - ta - nay,

Ho, ho, ___ Wa - ta - nay, Ho, ho, ___ Wa - ta - nay, Ki - yo - ke - na, Ki -

yo - ke - na. Ho, ho, ___ Wa - ta - nay, Ho, ho, ___ Wa - ta - nay,

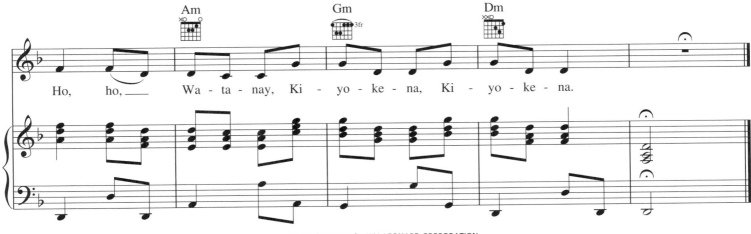

Ho, ho, ___ Wa - ta - nay, Ki - yo - ke - na, Ki - yo - ke - na.

JAMAICA FAREWELL

Traditional Caribbean

Down the way where the
Down at the mar- ket ___
Down by the wa- ter ___

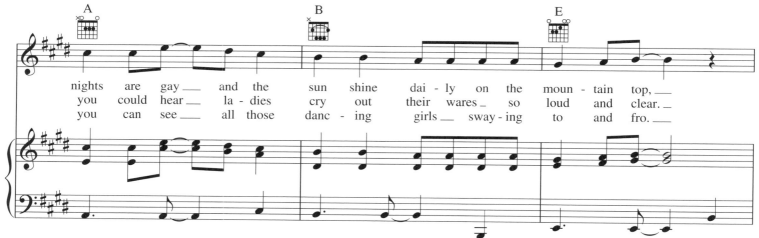

nights are gay ___ and the sun shine dai- ly on the moun- tain top, ___
you could hear ___ la- dies cry out their wares __ so loud and clear. __
you can see ___ all those danc- ing girls ___ sway- ing to and fro. ___

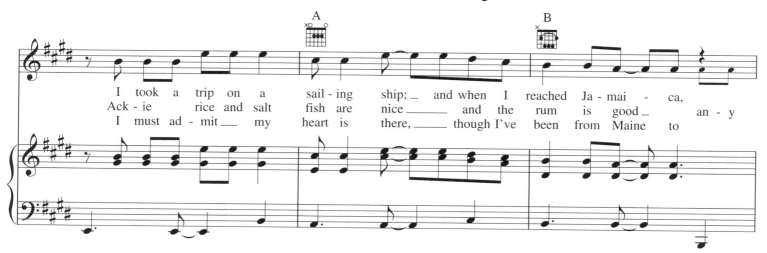

I took a trip on a sail- ing ship; __ and when I reached Ja- mai- ca,
Ack- ie rice and salt fish are nice ____ and the rum is good __ an- y
I must ad- mit __ my heart is there, ____ though I've been from Maine to

I made a stop.
time __ of year. } But I'm sad to say I'm on my way. __
Mex - i - co.

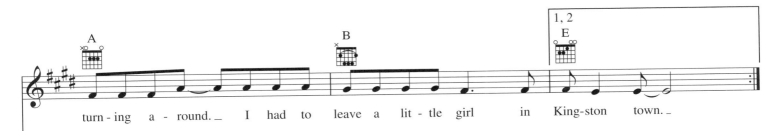

Won't be back for man - y a day. __ My heart is down, my head is

turn - ing a - round. __ I had to leave a lit - tle girl in King - ston town. __

King - ston town. __ I had to leave a lit - tle girl in King - ston town.

JEG LAGDE MIG SAA SILDE
(I Laid Me Down to Rest)

Norwegian Folk Song

Moderately

Jeg lag - de meg så sil - de alt sent om en
gan - ger jeg meg opp i hø - yen
gikk jeg meg ut på - den grøn - ne

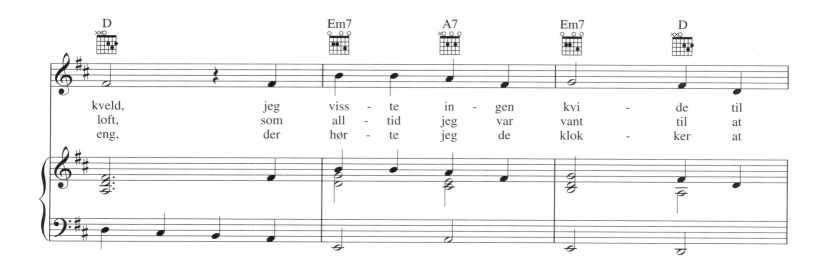

kveld, jeg viss - te in - gen kvi - de til
loft, som all - tid jeg var vant til at
eng, der hør - te jeg de klok - ker at

a have; så dom der da
gjø - re; der stan - der de
rin - ge; ei an - net jeg

bud   i - fra   kjæ -   res - ten   min,   jeg
jom - fru - er   alt _____ u - ti   flokk   og
vis - ste, ei   an - net   jeg for - nam,   enn

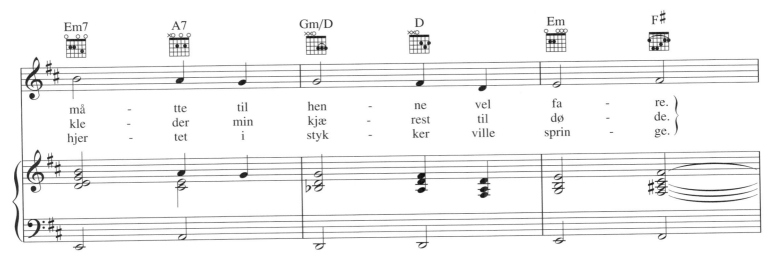

må -   tte   til   hen - ne   vel   fa -   re.
kle -   der   min   kjæ - rest   til   dø -   de.
hjer -   tet   i   styk - ker   ville sprin - ge.

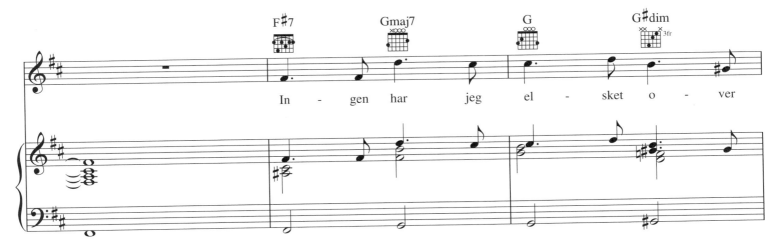

In - gen   har   jeg   el - sket o - ver

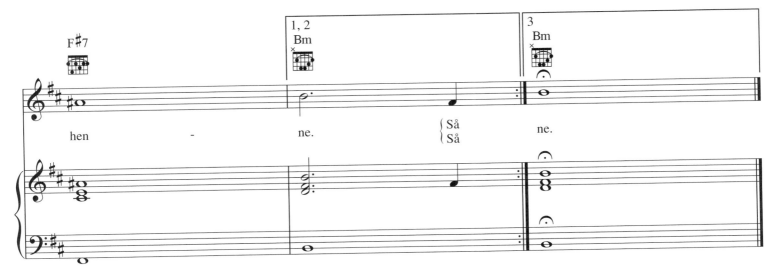

hen -   ne.   Så   ne.
                       Så

THE KEEL ROW

Northumbrian Folk Song

KEHTO LAULA

Finnish Folk Song

KRAKOWIAK
(Darling Maiden, Hark, I Ask Thee)

Polish Folk Song

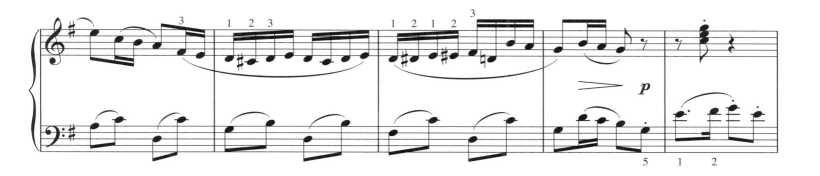

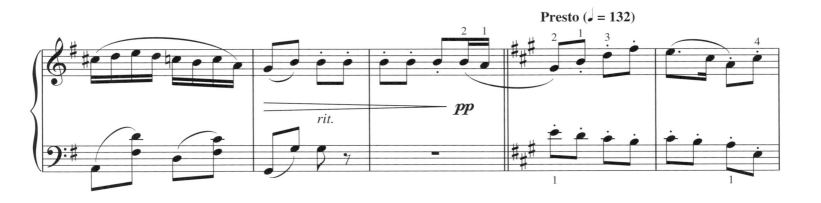

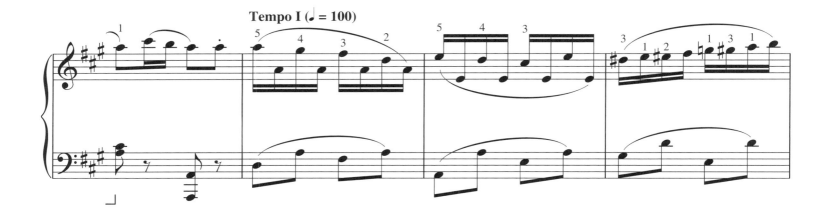

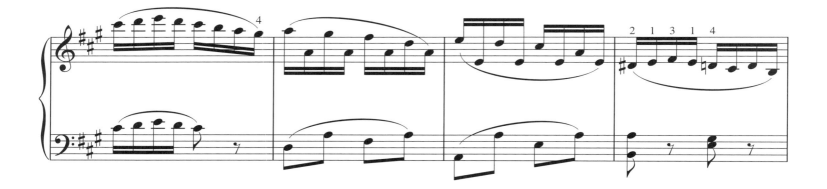

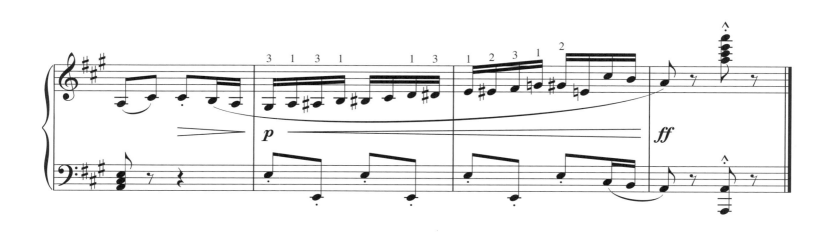

KOMORIUTA
(Lullaby)

Japanese Folk Song

LA CUCARACHA

Mexican Revolutionary Folk Song

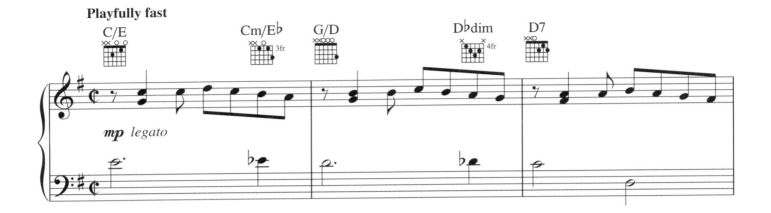

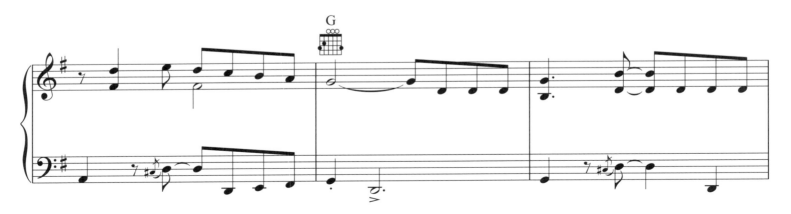

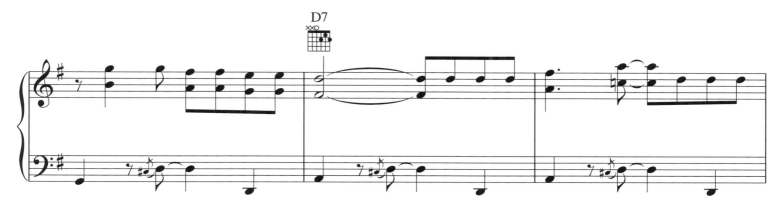

LITTLE SANDY GIRL

Tobago Folk Song

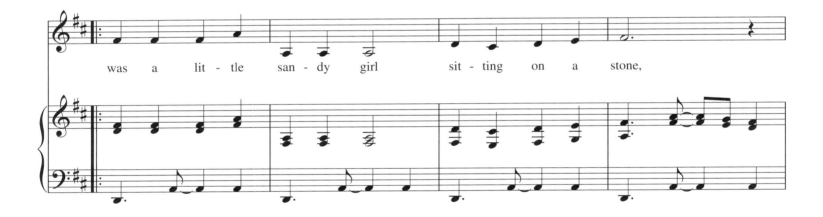

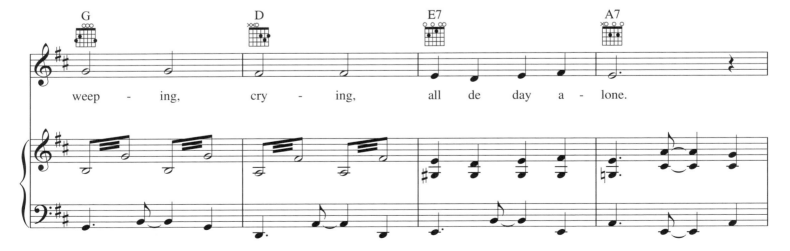

Rise up, san - dy girl, wipe your tears a -

way. Choose de one you love de best and

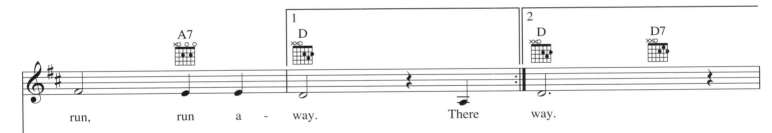

run, run a - way. There way.

Choose de one you love de best and run, run a - way.

MAGASAN REPÜL A DARÙ
(Hungaria's Treasure)

Hungarian Folk Song

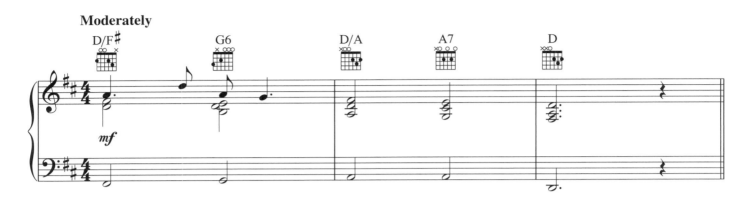

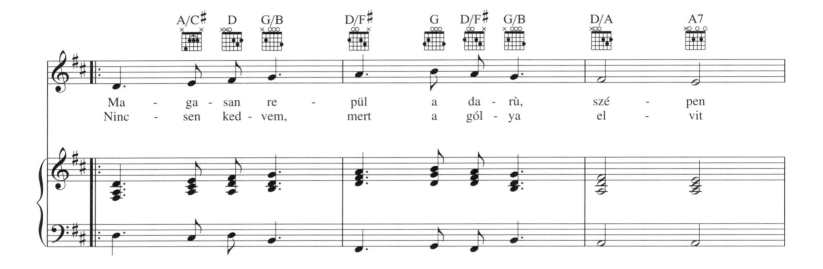

Ma - ga - san re - pül a da - rù, szé - pen
Ninc - sen ked - vem, mert a gól - ya el - vit

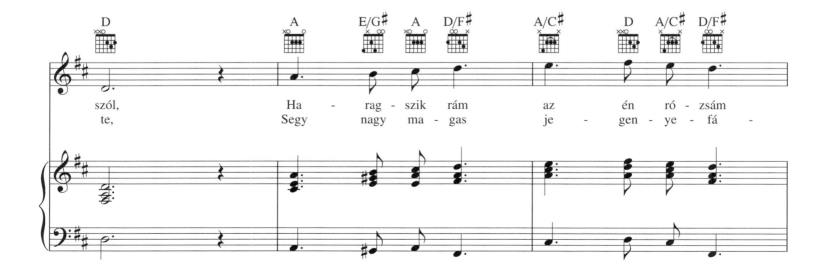

szól, Ha - rag - szik rám az én ró - zsám
te, Segy nagy ma - gas je - gen - ye - fá -

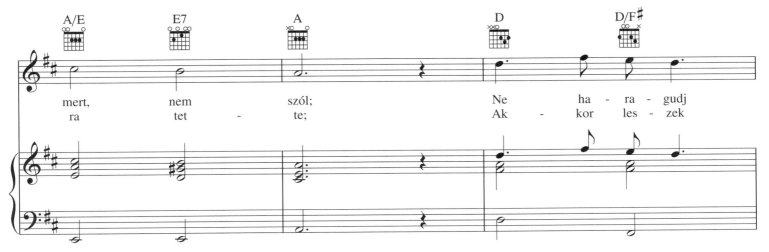

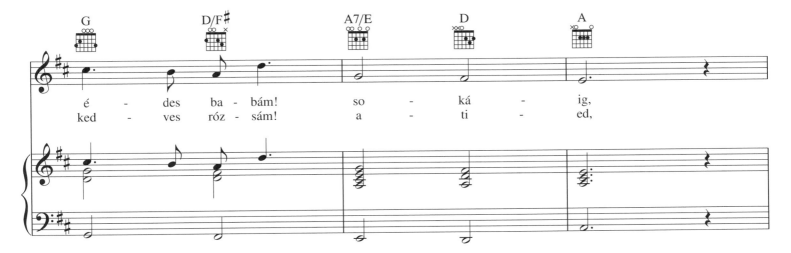

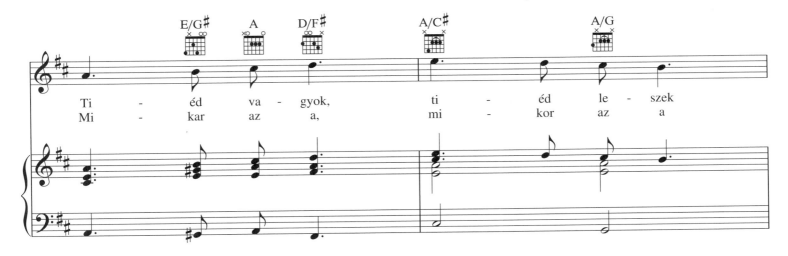

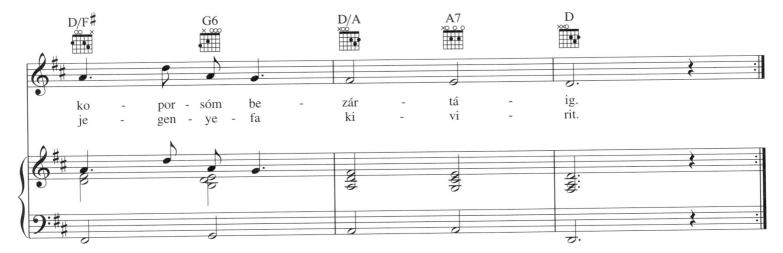

MAQUERÚLE

Traditional Colombian Folk Song

Moderately fast

Ma- que- rú- le e- ra un chom- bo, pa- na- de- ro de An- da- go-
rú- le no es- tá a- quí, Ma- que- rú- le es- tá en Con- do-
ru- le a ma- sa el pan, y lo ven- de de con- ta-

- ya, lo lla- ma- ban Ma- que- rú- le, se a- rrui-
- to, cuan- do ven- ga Ma- que- rú- le, su mu-
- do, Ma- que- rú- le ya no quie- re, que su

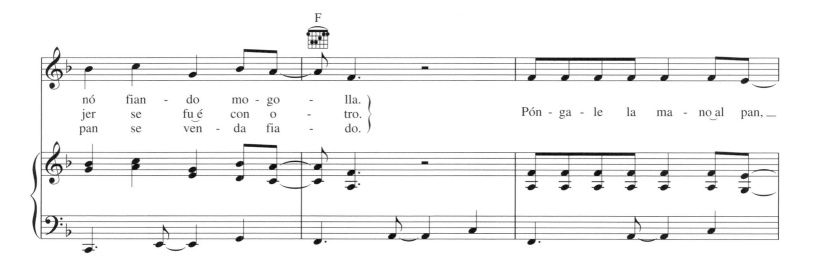

nó fian- do mo- go- lla.
jer se fué con o- tro.
pan se ven- da fia- do.

Pón- ga- le la ma- no al pan,

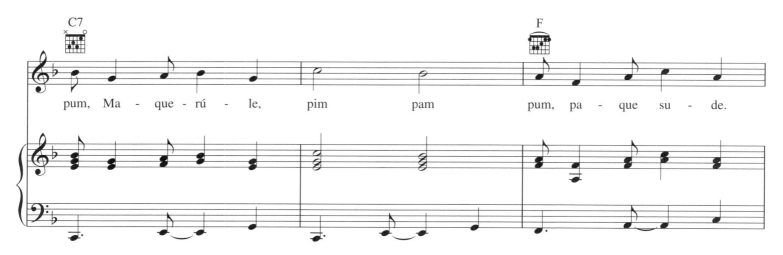

KUM BA YAH

Traditional Spiritual

MATILDA

Traditional Folk Song

Calypso beat

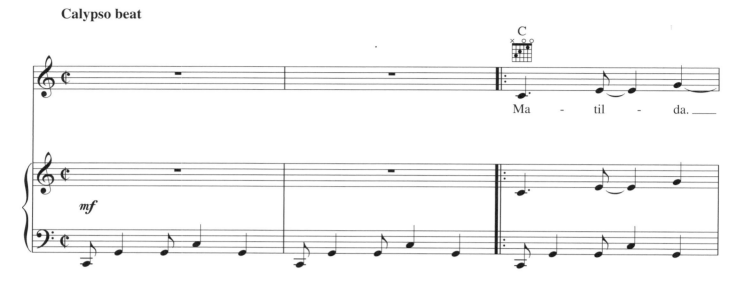

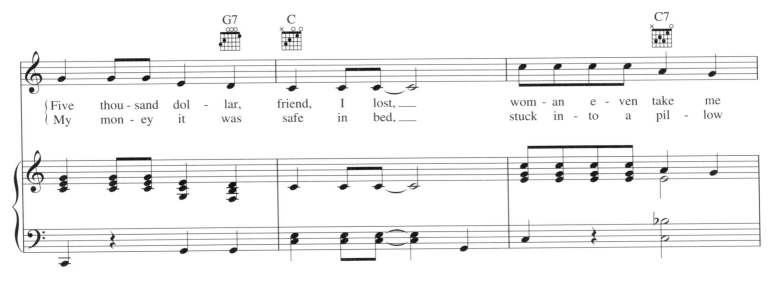

Five thou-sand dol-lar, friend, I lost, ___ wom-an e-ven take me
My mon-ey it was safe in bed, ___ stuck in-to a pil-low

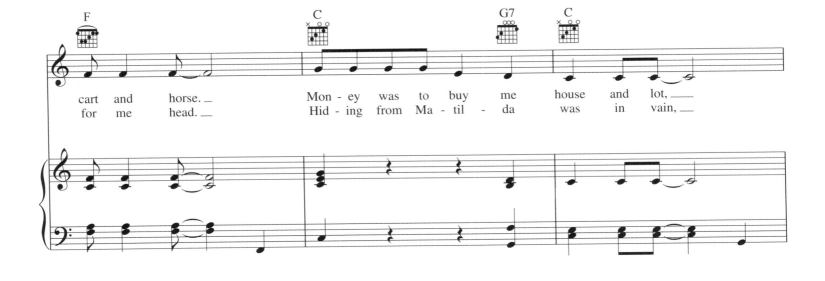

cart and horse. ___ Mon-ey was to buy me house and lot, ___
for me head. ___ Hid-ing from Ma-til-da was in vain, ___

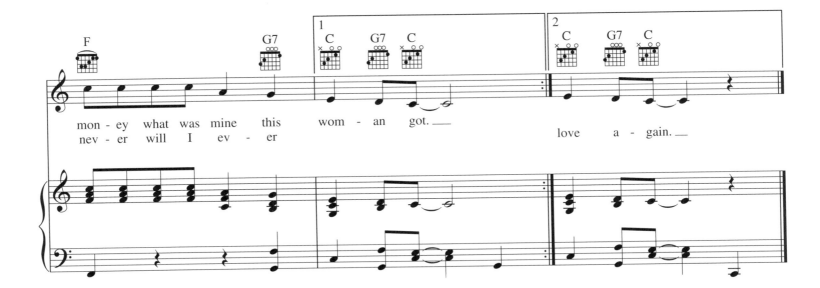

mon-ey what was mine this wom-an got. ___
nev-er will I ev-er love a-gain. ___

MEXICAN HAT DANCE
(Jarabe Topatio)

By F.A. PARTICHELA

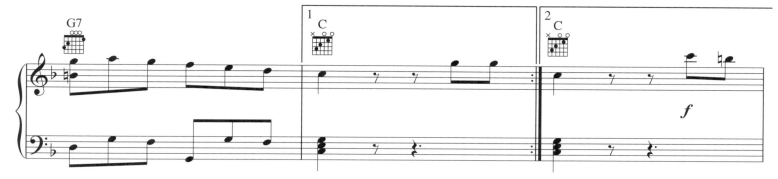

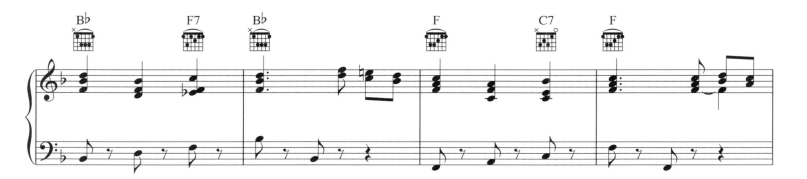

Tempo I

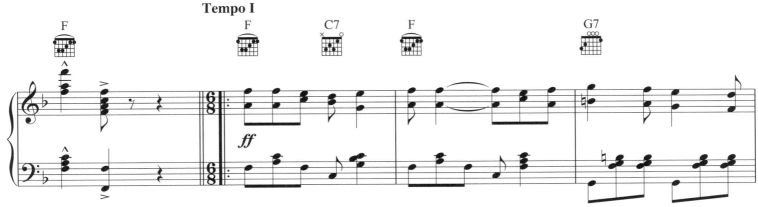

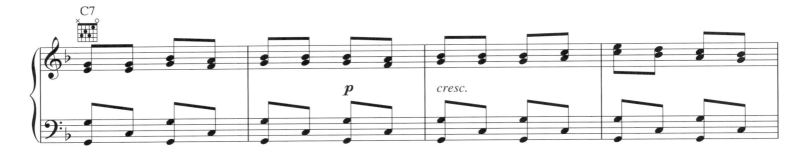

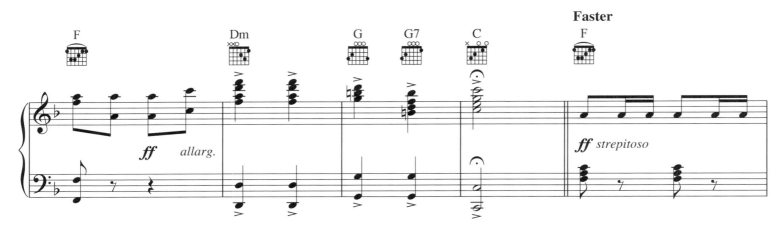

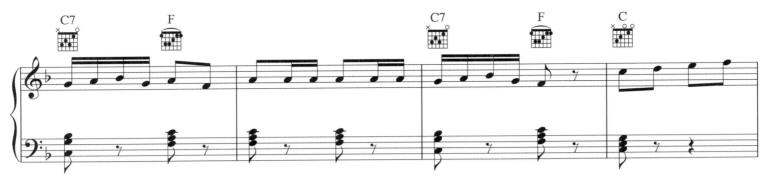

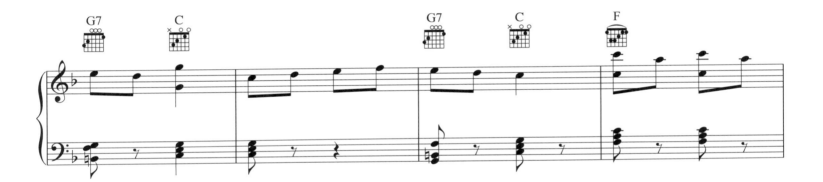

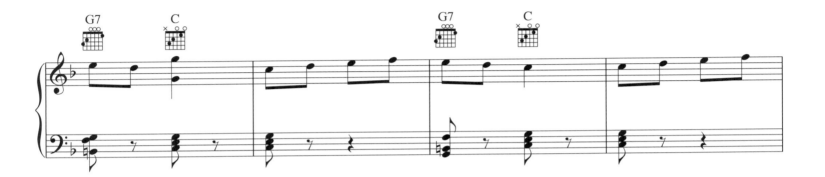

MI CABALLO BLANCO
(My White Horse)

Chilean Folk Song

fiel.
vó.
ré.

Mi ca - ba - llo, mi ca - ba - llo,

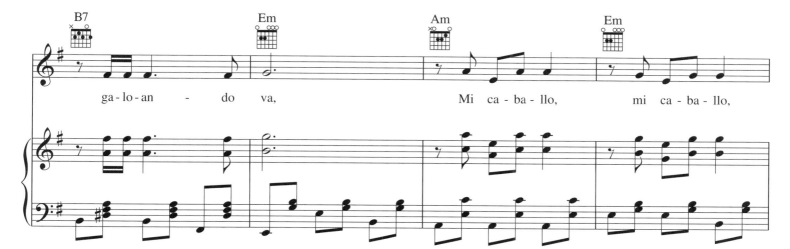

ga - lo - an - do va, Mi ca - ba - llo, mi ca - ba - llo,

se va y se va. Ah, _____ ah, _____

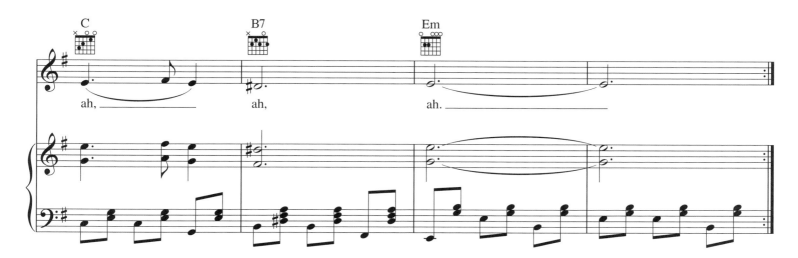

ah, _____ ah, ah. _____

NASSAU BOUND

Bahaman Sea Chanty

There's no bet-ter place ___ than a

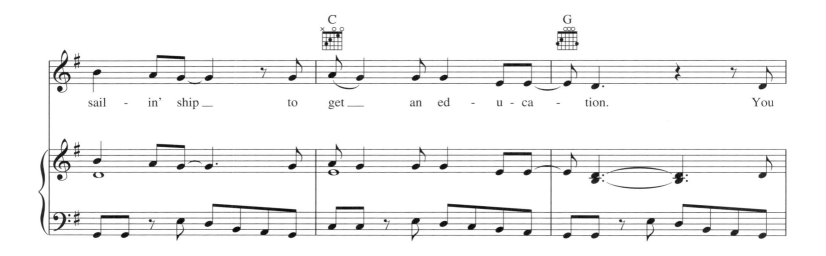

sail-in' ship ___ to get ___ an ed-u-ca-tion. You

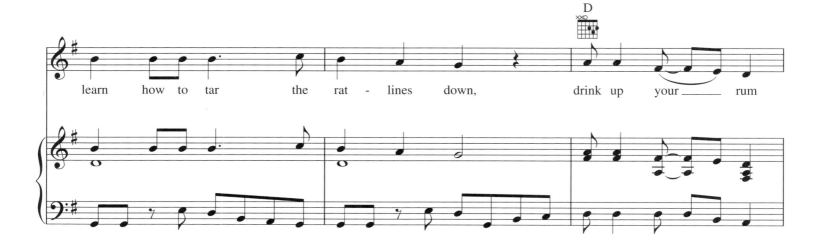

learn how to tar the rat-lines down, drink up your ___ rum

ra - tion. _____ So, hoist up the John B's

sails, see how the main - sail sets.

Call for the Cap - tain a - shore, let ___ me go home.

Let me go home, let ___ me go

home. I feel so break _ up,

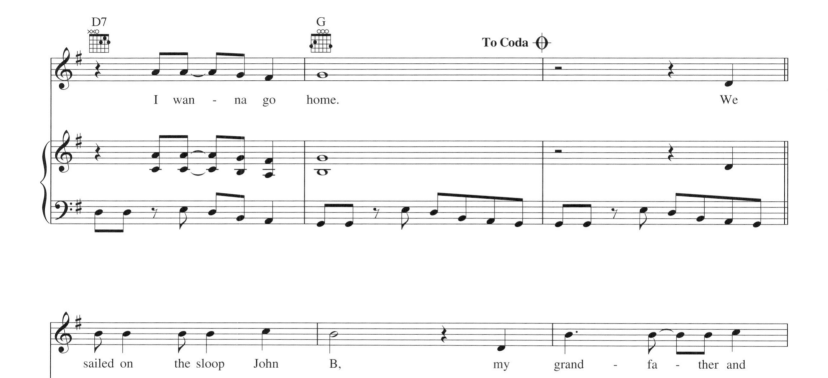

I wan - na go home. We

sailed on the sloop John B, my grand - fa - ther and

me, a - round Nas - sau town _ we _ did

roam. Drink-in' all night, got in - to a

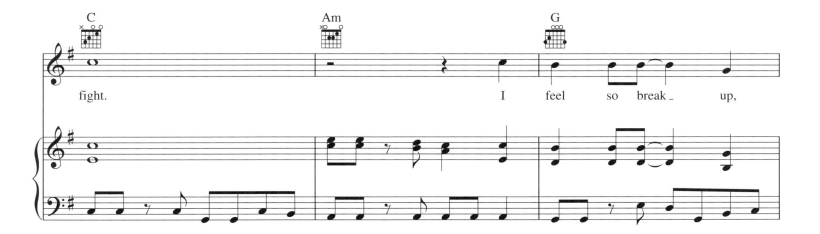

fight. I feel so break _ up,

I wan - na go home. We

car - ried the la - dies to Nas - sau town, _ like oth - er sail - in'
eat a - board _ the _____ sloop John B, _____ food of the ver - y

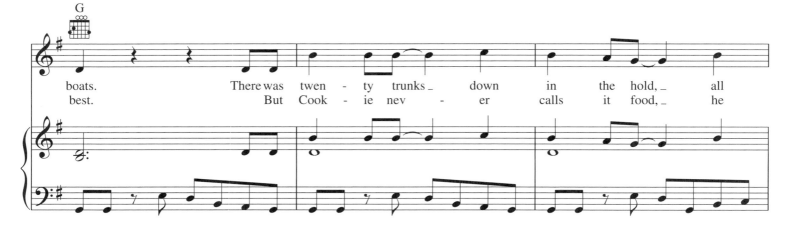

boats. There was twen - ty trunks_ down in the hold,_ all
best. But Cook - ie nev - er calls it food,_ he

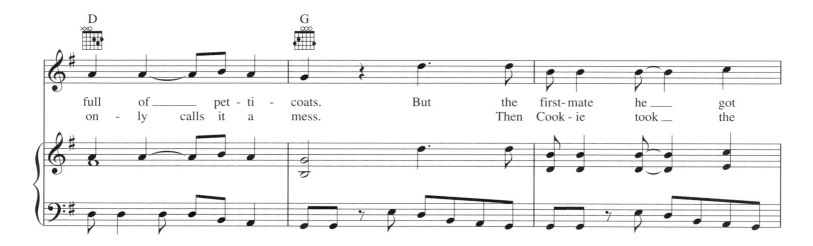

full of _____ pet - ti - coats. But the first-mate he ____ got
on - ly calls it a mess. Then Cook - ie he took ____ the

drunk, broke up the la - dies' trunks. The
fits, throw'way all ___ the grits.

con - sta - ble come on board ___ to take him a - way.
Then he took and throw 'way ___ all ___ of the corn.

Sher-iff John Stone, let ___ me a - lone.
Let me go home, let ___ me go home.

I feel so break ___ up, I wan - na go
I feel so break ___ up, I wan - na go

home. We
home. Oh, there's

D.S. al Coda

CODA

I feel so break ___ up, I wan - na go home.

NING WENDETE

Kenyan Folk Song

Moderately fast

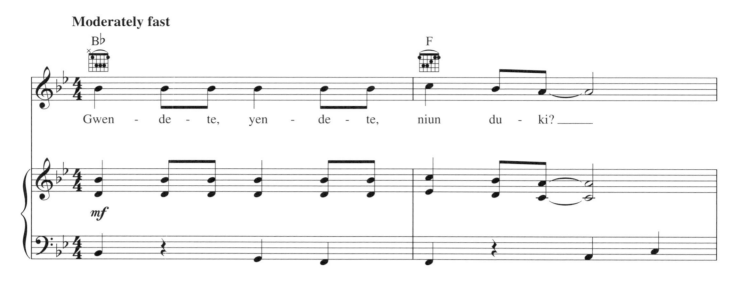

Gwen - de - te, yen - de - te, niun du - ki? _____

Gwen - de - te, dun - yen - de - te, niun du - ki? _____

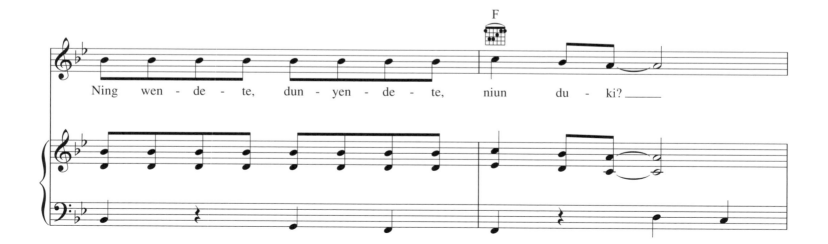

Ning wen - de - te, dun - yen - de - te, niun du - ki? _____

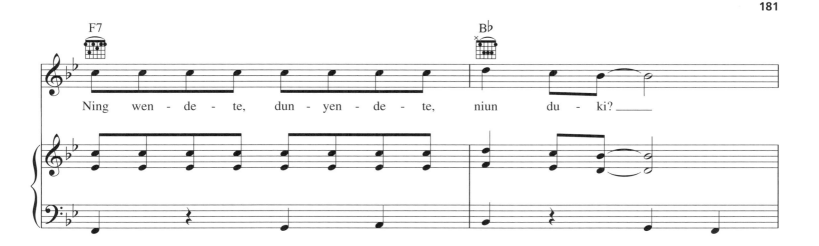

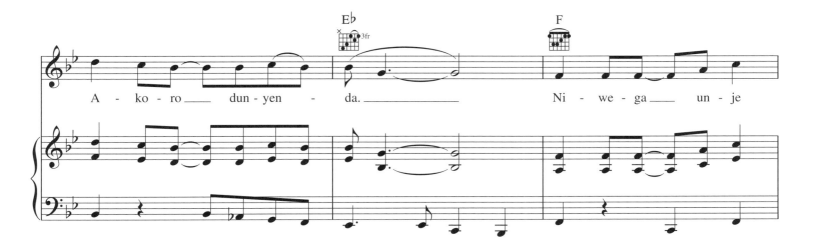

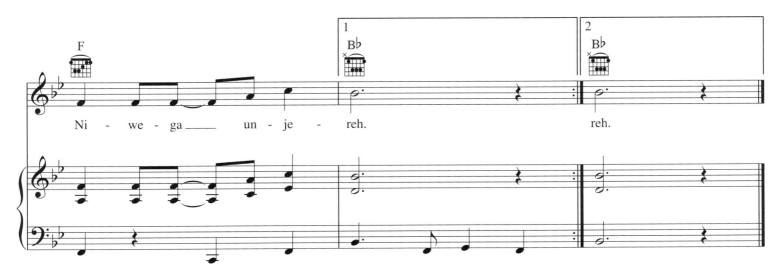

NONA MANIS

Indonesian Folk Song

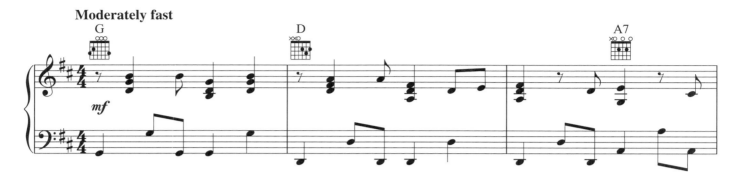

Moderately fast

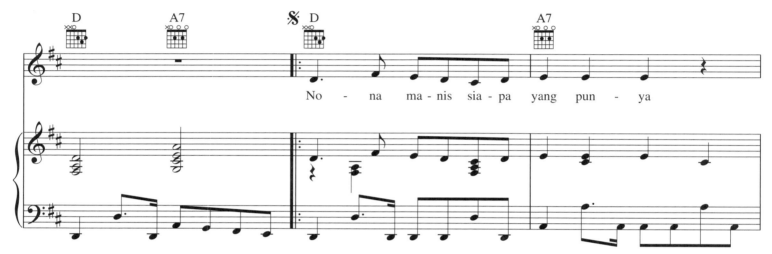

No - na ma - nis sia - pa yang pun - ya

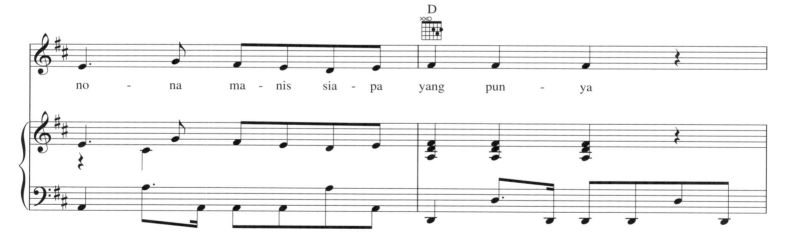

no - na ma - nis sia - pa yang pun - ya

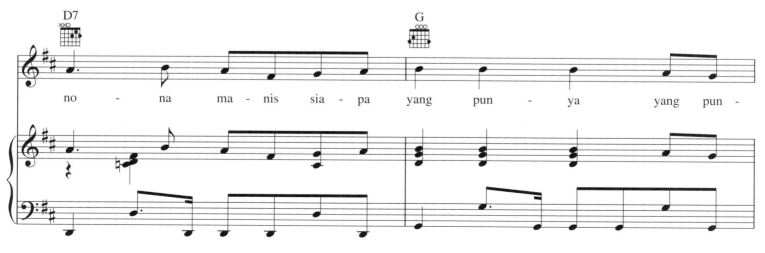

no - na ma - nis sia - pa yang pun - ya yang pun -

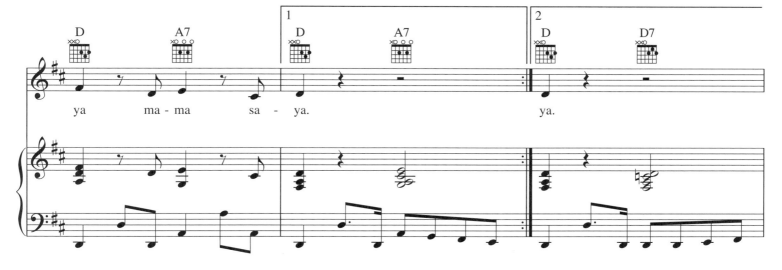

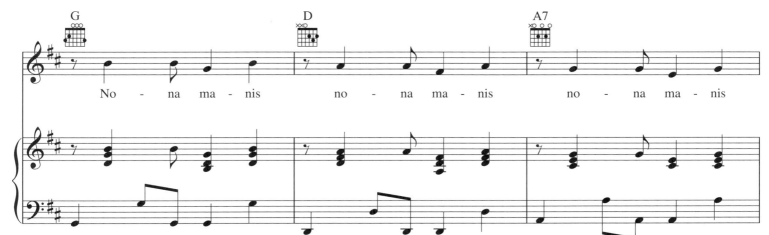

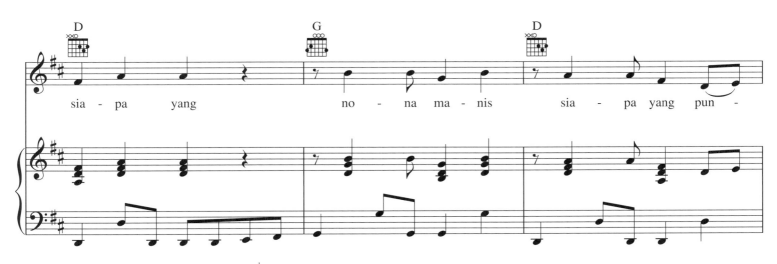

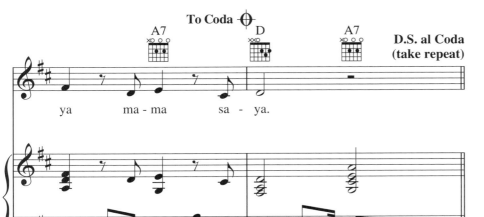

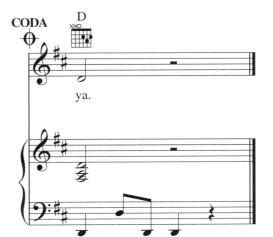

MARIANNE

Traditional

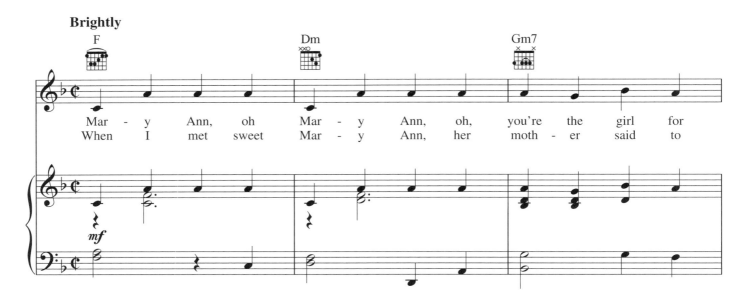

Brightly

Mar-y Ann, oh Mar-y Ann, oh, you're the girl for
When I met sweet Mar-y Ann, her moth-er said to

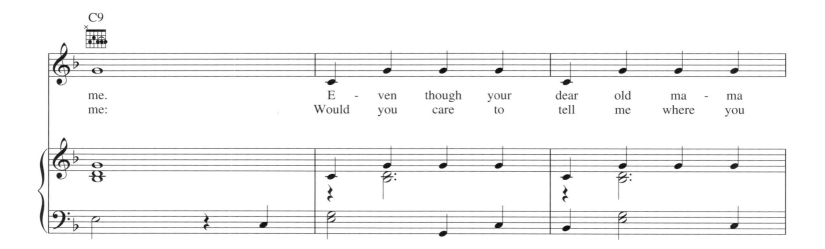

me. E-ven though your dear old ma-ma
me: Would you care to tell me where you

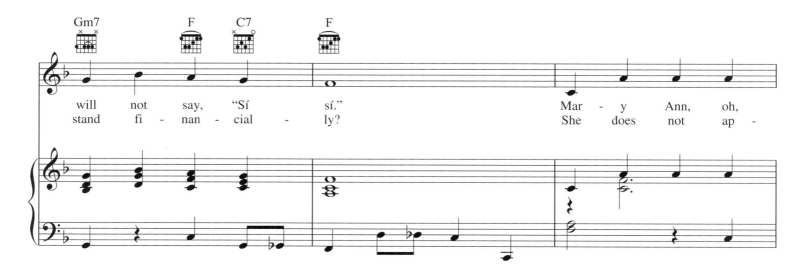

will not say, "Sí sí." Mar-y Ann, oh,
stand fi-nan-cial-ly? She does not ap-

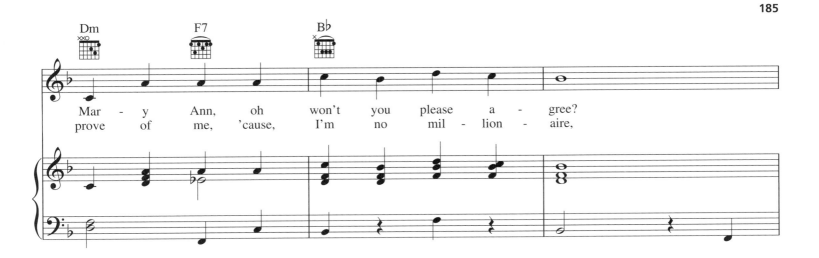

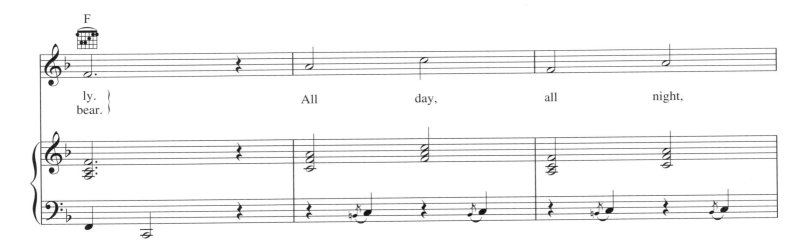

sea - side sift - in' sand, ____

all the lit - tle chil - dren love Mar - y Ann, ____

____ down by the sea - side

sift - in' sand. ____

NORWEGIAN DANCE

By EDVARD GRIEG

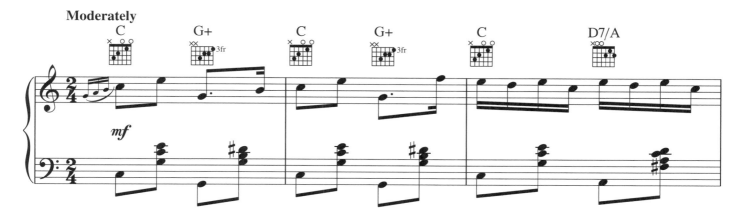

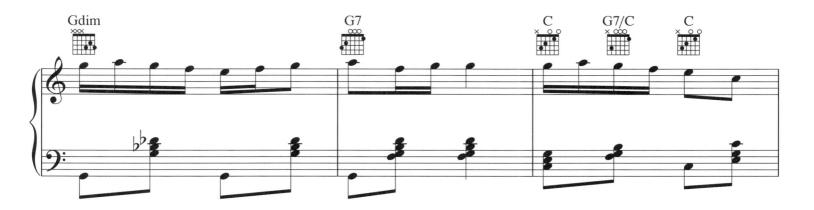

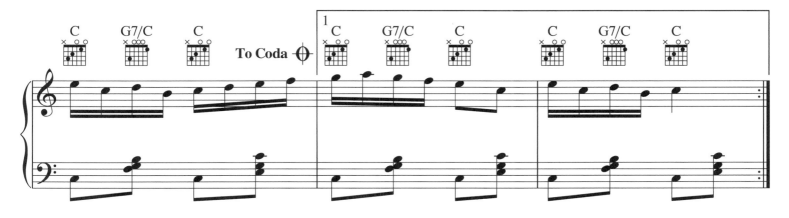

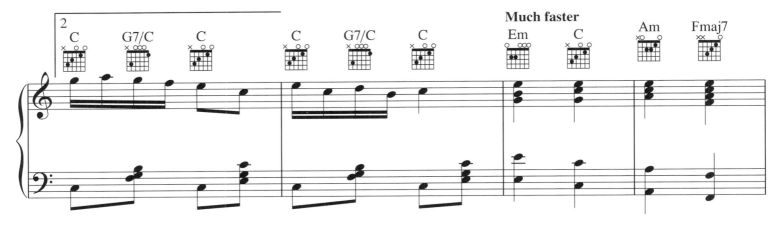

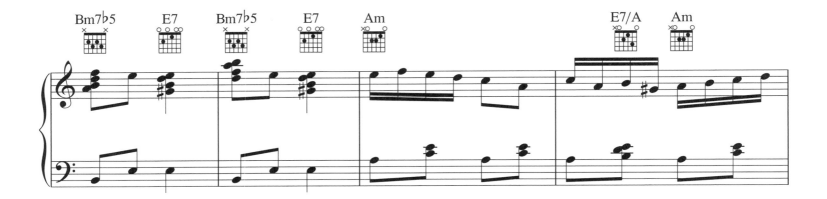

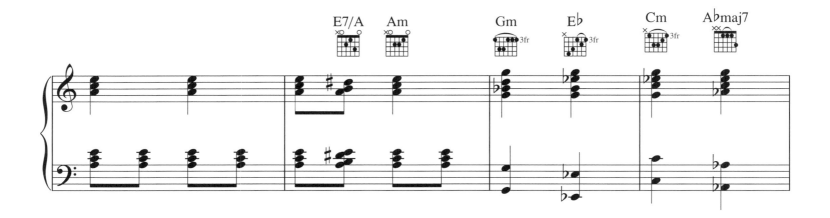

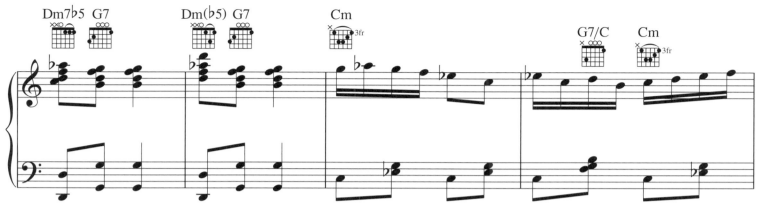

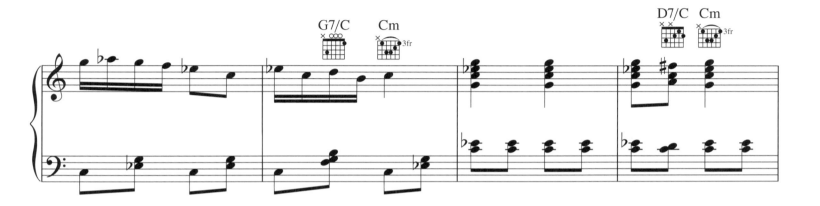

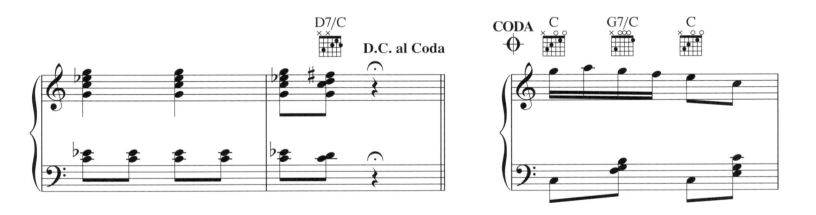

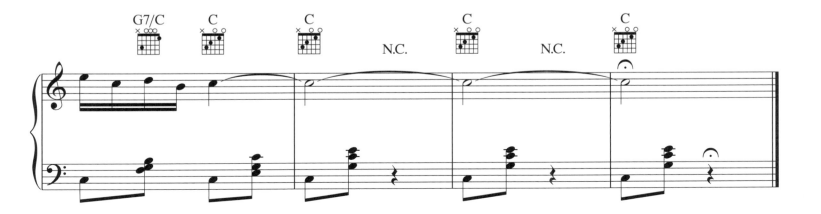

PARUPARONG BUKID
(The Butterfly Field)

Traditional Filipino Folk Song

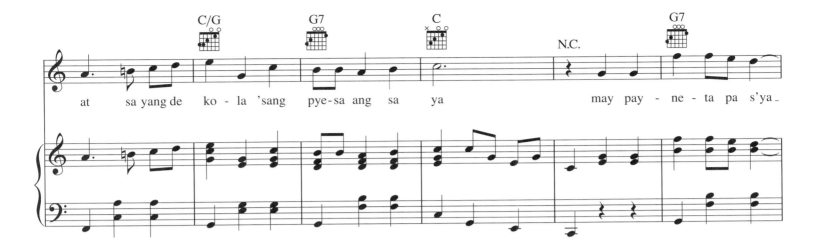

at sa yang de ko - la 'sang pye-sa ang sa ya may pay - ne - ta pa s'ya

may suk - lay pa - man-din nag - was de O - he - tes ang pa -

la - la - ba - sin Ha - ha - rap sa al - tar at ma - na - na - la - min at sa - ka la -

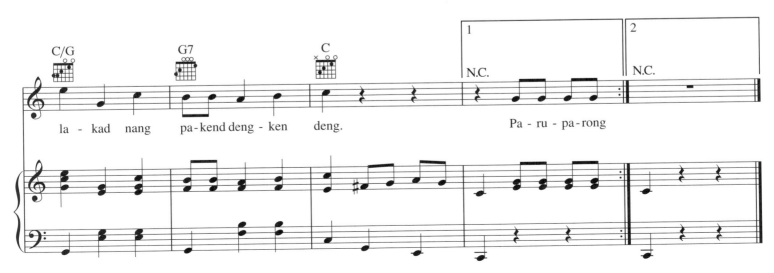

la - kad nang pa - kend deng - ken deng. Pa - ru - pa - rong

PAT-A-PAN
(Willie, Take Your Little Drum)

Words and Music by
BERNARD de la MONNOYE

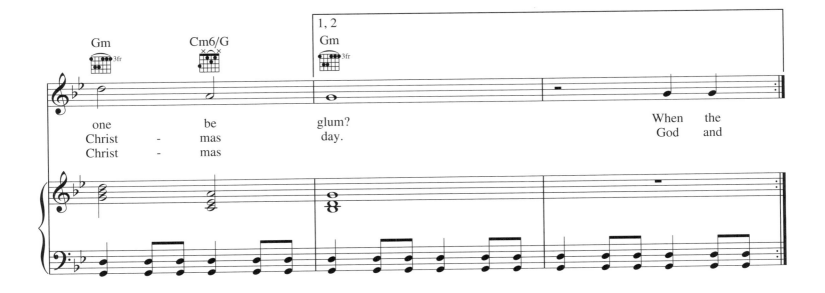

PETE, PETE

West African Folk Song

Moderately fast

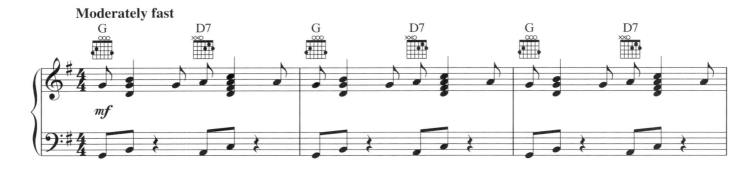

mf

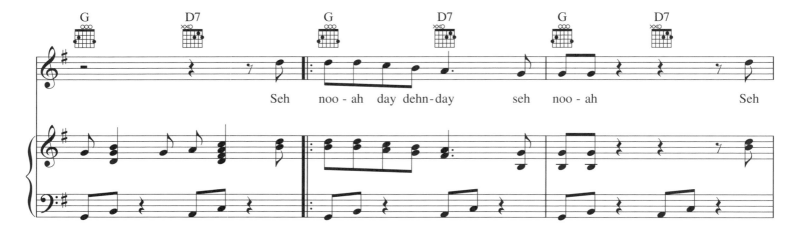

Seh noo - ah day dehn-day   seh noo - ah   Seh

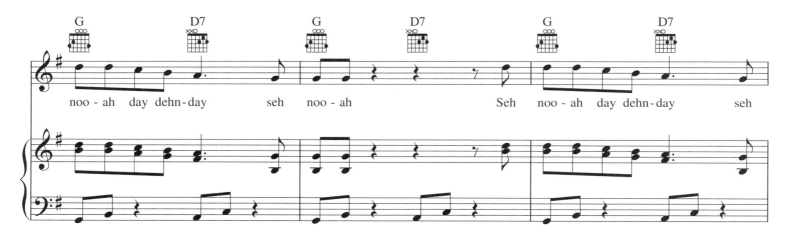

noo - ah day dehn-day   seh noo - ah   Seh noo - ah day dehn-day   seh

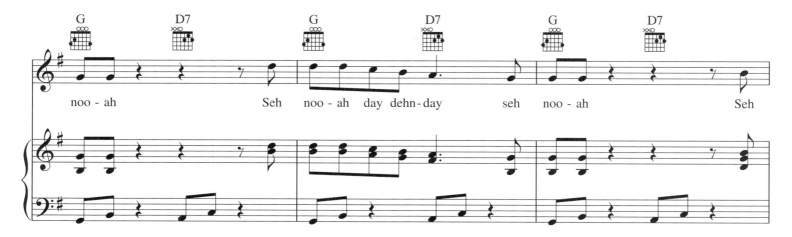

noo - ah   Seh noo - ah day dehn-day   seh noo - ah   Seh

THE OVERLANDER
(The Queensland Drover)

Australian Folk Song

Moderately

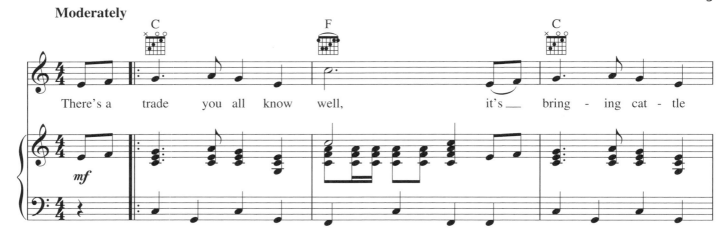

There's a trade you all know well, it's __ bring - ing cat - tle

o - ver. On __ ev - 'ry track to the gulf and back, men know the Queens-land Dro - ver.

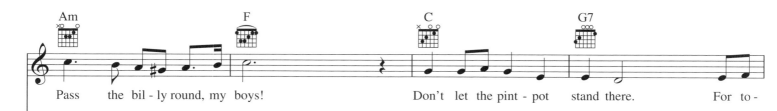

Pass the bil - ly round, my boys! Don't let the pint - pot stand there. For to-

night we drink the health of ev - 'ry O - ver - land - er. There's a land - er.

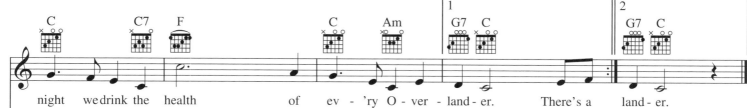

PJESMA
(Come, My Dearest)

Serbian Folk Song

Moderately fast

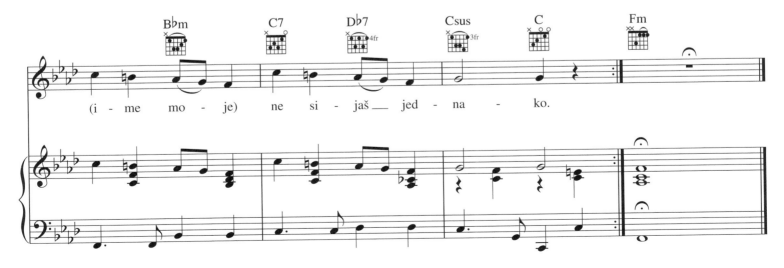

RASA SAYANG EH
(Oh, To Be in Love)

Malaysian Folk Song

Ra - sa sa - yang eh, ra - sa sa - yang sa - yang eh. Eh

li - hat no - na jauh, __ ra - sa sa - yang sa - yang eh. Ra - sa Sa - yang eh, ra - sa

sa - yang sa - yang eh. Eh li - hat no - na jauh, __ ra - sa sa - yang sa - yang eh.

Ra - sa

There are no formal lyrics for the verses. You can improvise, using the melody as a guide.

RIO, RIO

Chilean Folk Song

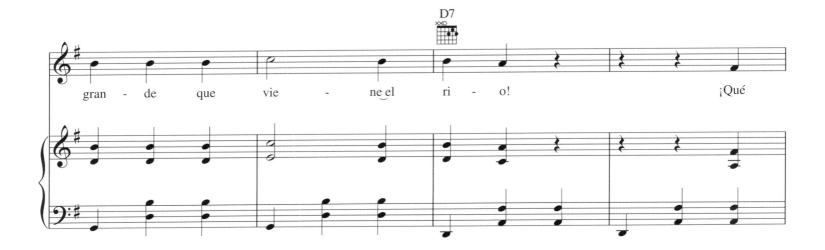

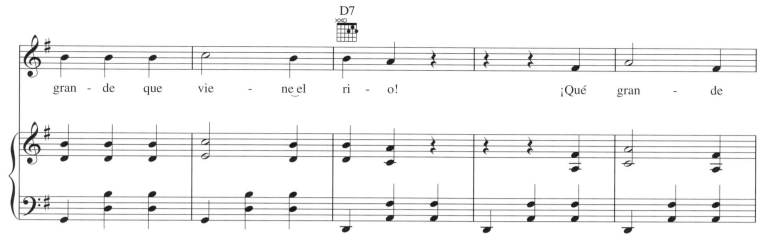

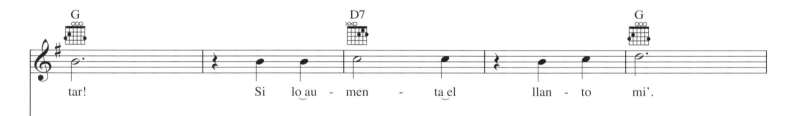

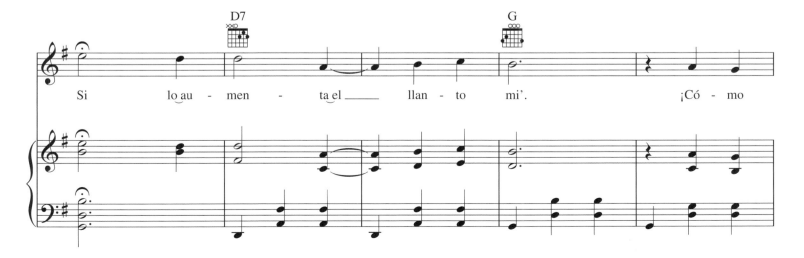

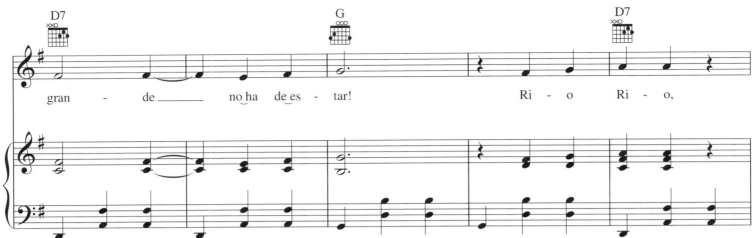

gran - de _____ no ha de es - tar! Ri - o Ri - o,

Ri - o Ri - o, de - vol - véd - me el _____ a - mor

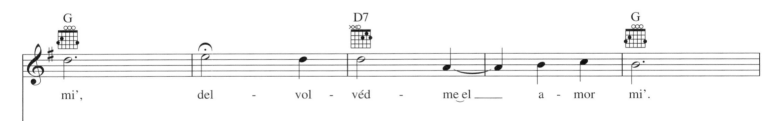

mi', del - vol - véd - me el _____ a - mor mi'.

Que me can - so _____ de llo - rar.

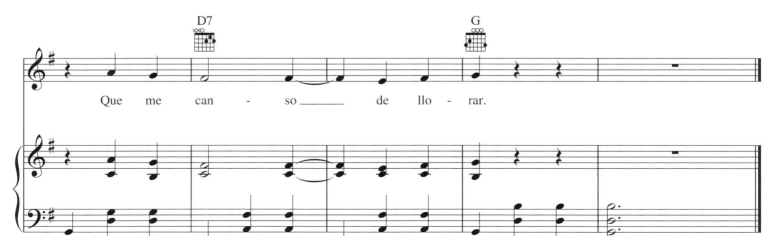

RA SI'LA MIELE
(Grind the Meal)

African Folk Song

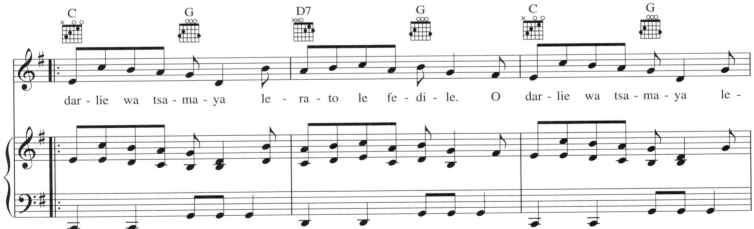

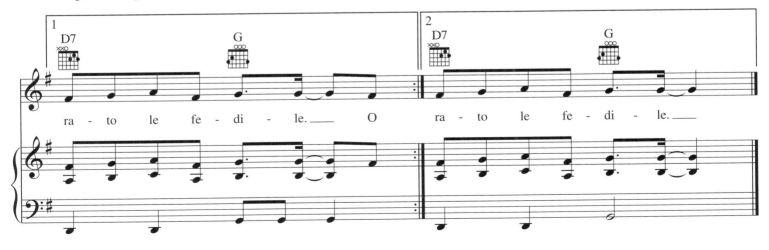

RIVERS OF BABYLON

Jamaican Folk Song

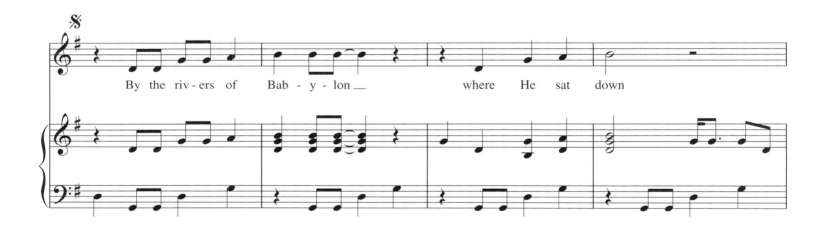

By the riv-ers of Bab-y-lon ___ where He sat down

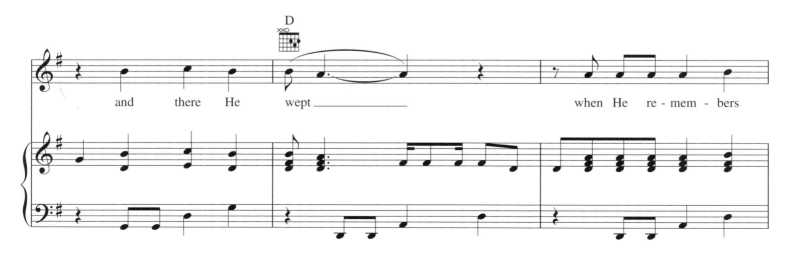

and there He wept ___ when He re-mem-bers

Zi - on. ___ 'Cause the wick - ed ___ car - ried us a - way, cap -

tiv - i - ty, ___ re - qui - red from us a song. ___ How ___

___ can we sing King of ___ our song ___ in a strange ___ land? ___

___ 'Cause the wick - ed ___ car - ried us a - way, cap -

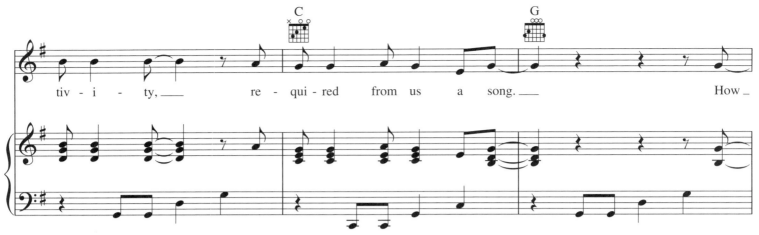

tiv - i - ty, ___ re - qui - red from us a song. ___ How ___

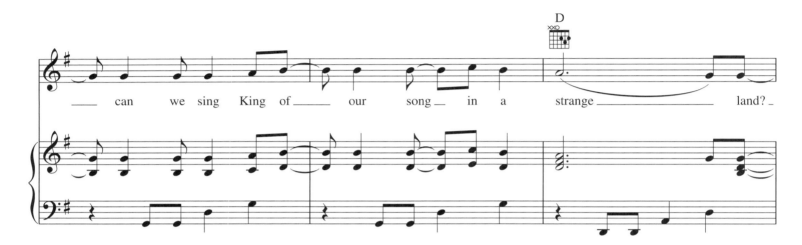

___ can we sing King of ___ our song ___ in a strange ___ land? ___

___ Sing it out loud. ___ (Ah.) ___ Sing a song of free-dom, { broth - er. / sis - ter. }

(Ah.) ___ Sing a song of free-dom, { bro - broth - er. ___ / sis - sis - ter. ___ }

Oh, _____ la la. (Ah ah ah ah) Mm. _____

(Ah.) _____ We gon-na {sing and shout it. / walk and talk it.} (Ah. _____

We gon-na {jump for joy. ___ / sing and shout. ___} Yeah, yeah, yeah. ___ Shout the song of free-dom

now. (Ah ah ah ah.) Whoa, __ whoa, _____ whoa. So let the

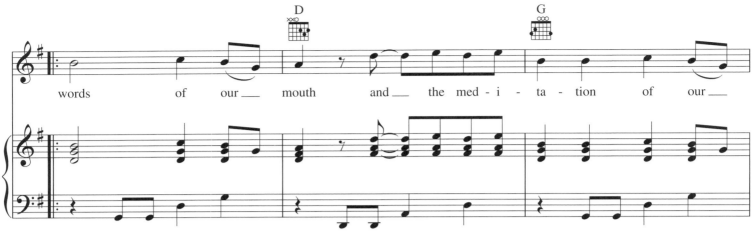

words of our mouth and the med-i-ta-tion of our

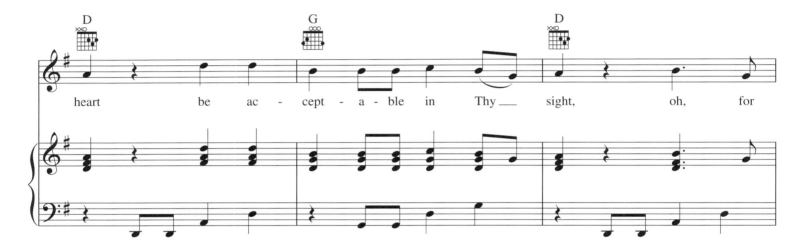

heart be ac-cept-a-ble in Thy sight, oh, for

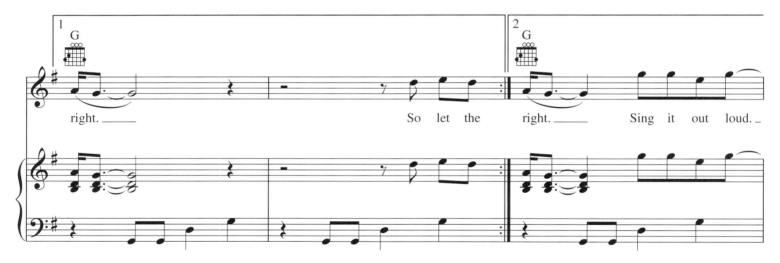

right. So let the right. Sing it out loud.

(Ah.) We got to sing it to-geth-er. (Ah.)

Ev-'ry-one of us. _____ (Ah ah ah ah.) La la la la la _____

la la. (Ah ah ah ah.) Whoa, __ whoa, _____ whoa. __ (Ah.) _____

(Ah.) _____

D.S. and Fade

Optional Ending

ROCKING

Traditional Czech Carol

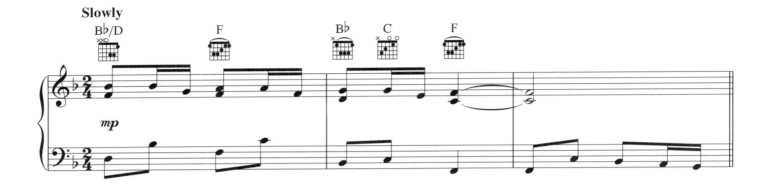

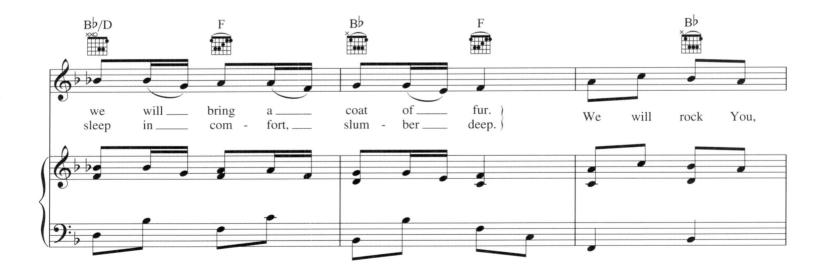

rock You, rock You. Gen - tly slum - ber as we rock You.

See the fur to keep You _____ warm,
We will praise to You all we _____ can,

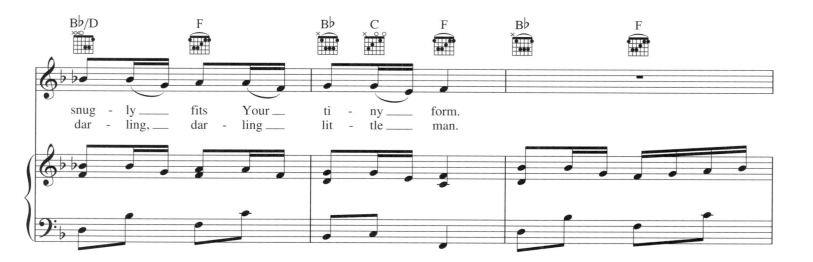

snug - ly _____ fits Your _ ti - ny _____ form.
dar - ling, _____ dar - ling _____ lit - tle _____ man.

ROSA

Flemish Dance Tune

Ro - sa, wil - len wy
Ro - sa, wil - len wy

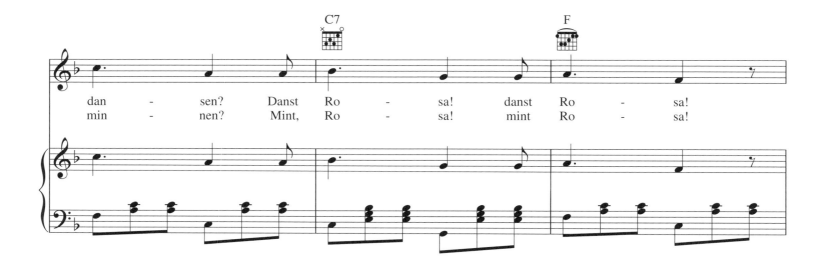

dan - sen? Danst Ro - sa! danst Ro - sa!
min - nen? Mint, Ro - sa! mint Ro - sa!

Ro - sa, wil - len wy dan - sen? Danst Ro - sa zoet! _____
Ro - sa, wil - len wy min - nen? Mint Ro - sa zoet! _____

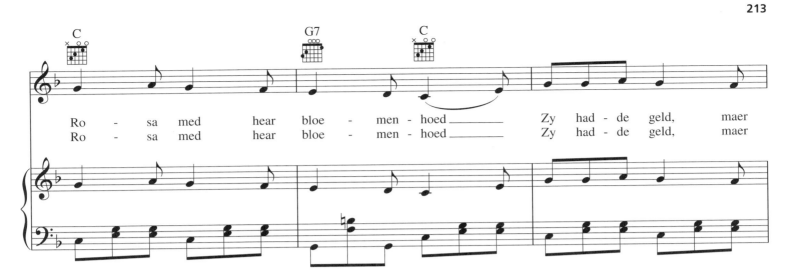

Ro - sa med hear bloe - men - hoed _____ Zy had - de geld, maer
Ro - sa med hear bloe - men - hoed _____ Zy had - de geld, maer

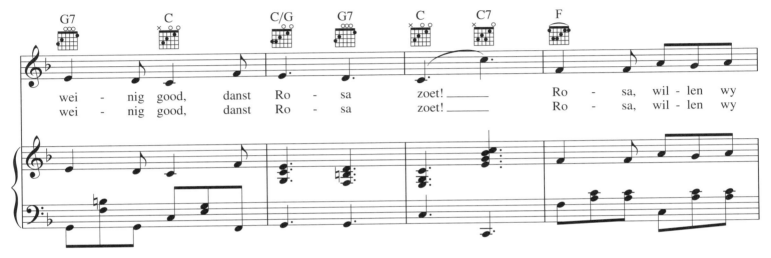

wei - nig good, danst Ro - sa zoet! _____ Ro - sa, wil - len wy
wei - nig good, danst Ro - sa zoet! _____ Ro - sa, wil - len wy

dan - sen? Danst Ro - sa! danst Ro - sa, Ro - sa, wil - len wy
min - nen? Mint Ro - sa! mint Ro - sa! Ro - sa, wil - len wy

dan - sen? Danst Ro - sa zoet!
min - nen? Mint Ro - sa zoet!

SAKURA
(Cherry Blossoms)

Traditional Japanese Folk Song

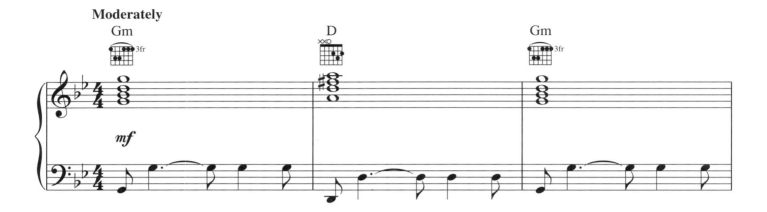

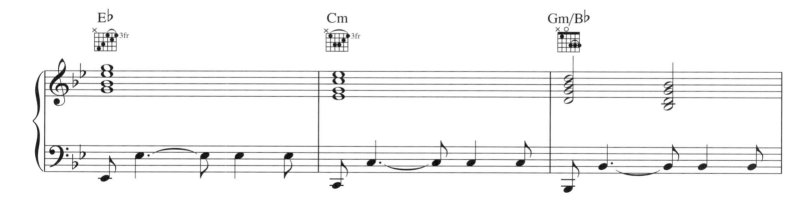

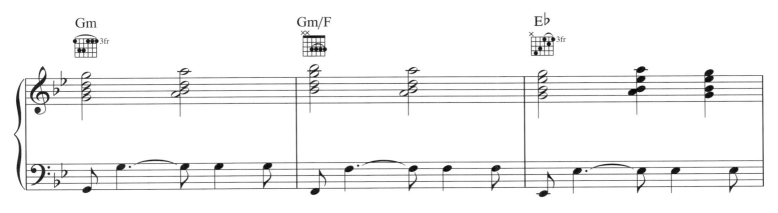

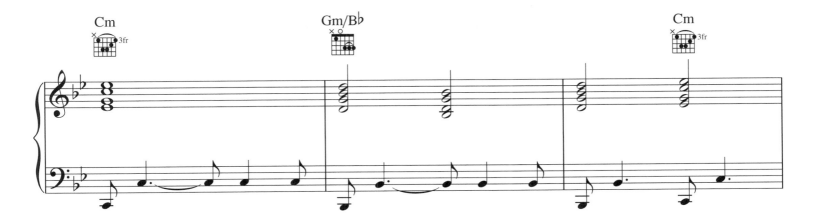

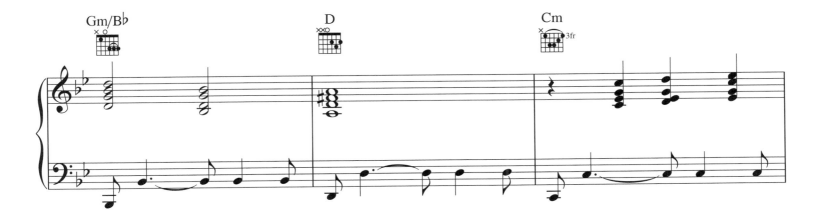

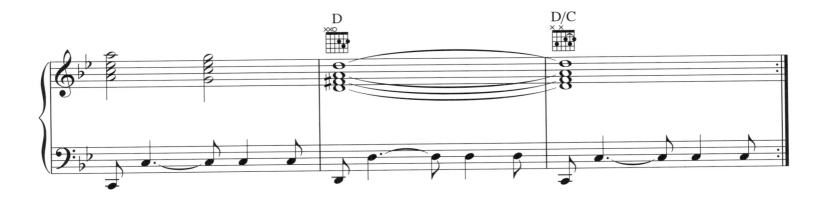

SHALOM CHAVERIM
(Shalom Friends)

Traditional Hebrew Singalong

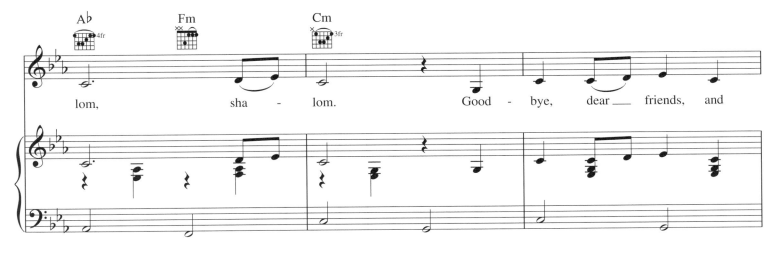

lom, sha - lom. Good - bye, dear __ friends, and

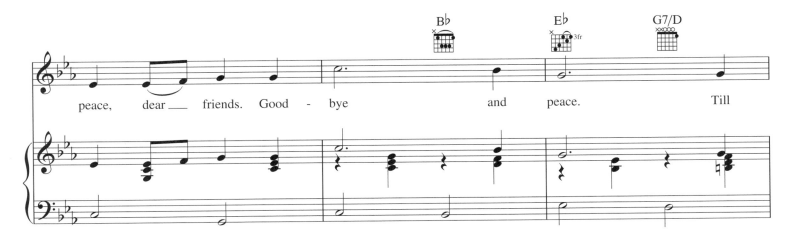

peace, dear __ friends. Good - bye and peace. Till

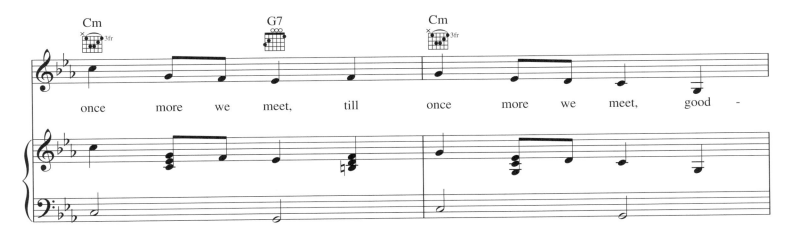

once more we meet, till once more we meet, good -

bye and __ peace. Sha - peace.

SHINING MOON

Traditional Thai Folk Song

Flowing

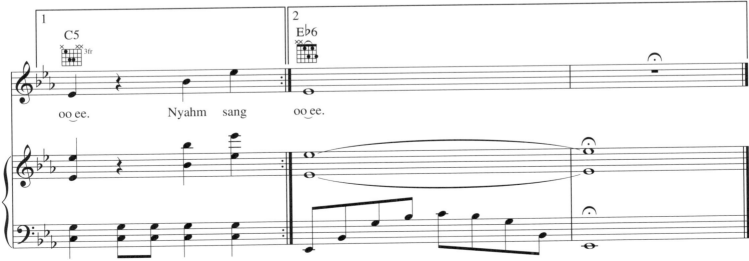

SINGABAHAMBAYO
(An Army Is Marching)

African Folk Song

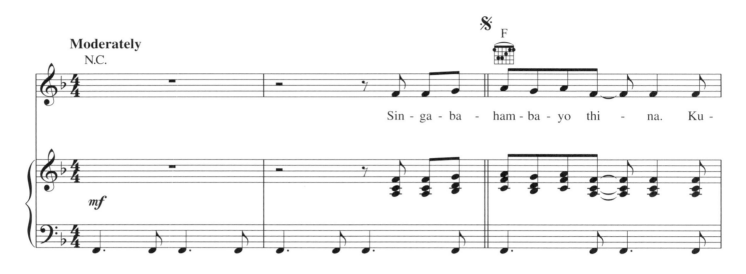

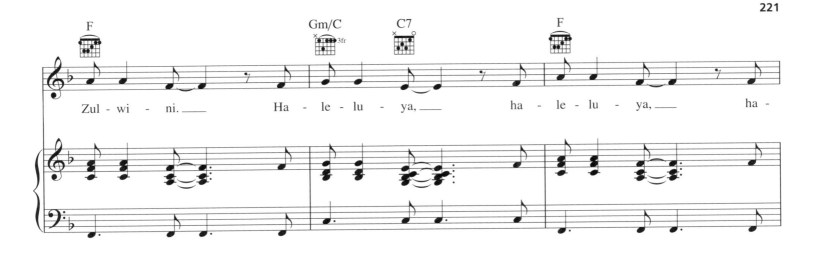

Zul - wi - ni. ___ Ha - le - lu - ya, ___ ha - le - lu - ya, ___ ha -

le - lu - ya, ha - le - lu - ya, ha - le - lu - ya. ___ Ha -

le - lu - ya, ___ ha - le - lu - ya, ___ ha - le - lu - ya, ha - le - lu - ya, ha -

le - lu - ya. ___ Oh, we are march - ing for free - dom, we're

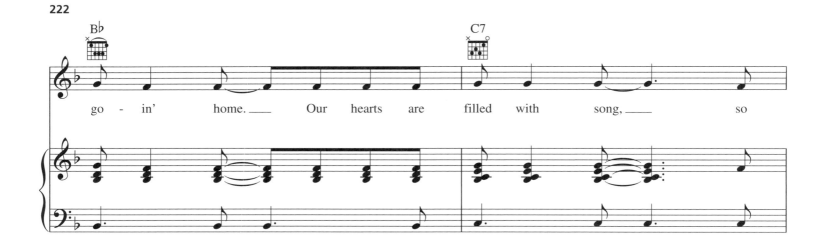

go - in' home. ___ Our hearts are filled with song, ___ so

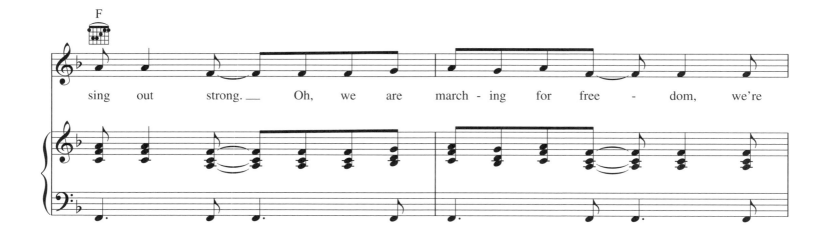

sing out strong. ___ Oh, we are march - ing for free - dom, we're

go - in' home. ___ Our hearts are filled with song, ___ so

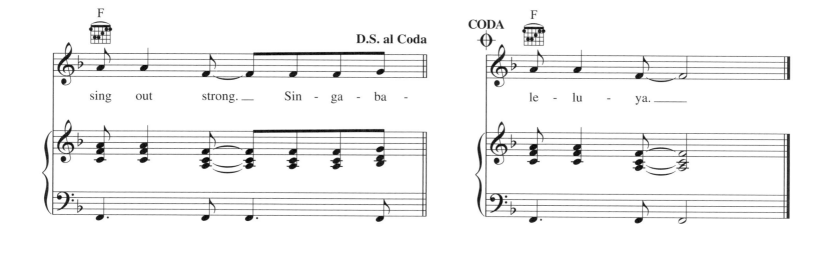

sing out strong. ___ Sin - ga - ba -

CODA

le - lu - ya. ___

D.S. al Coda

ROUXINOL DO PICO PRETO
(Nightingale with the Dark Beak)

Brazilian Folk Song

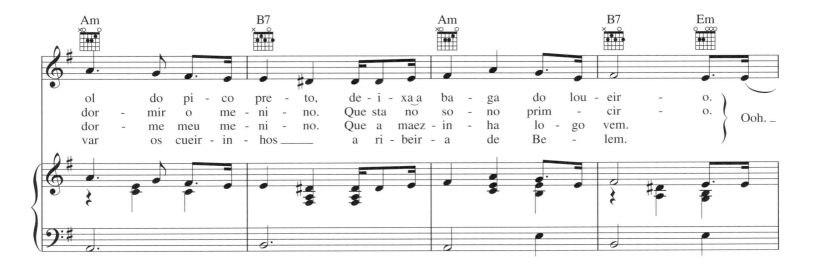

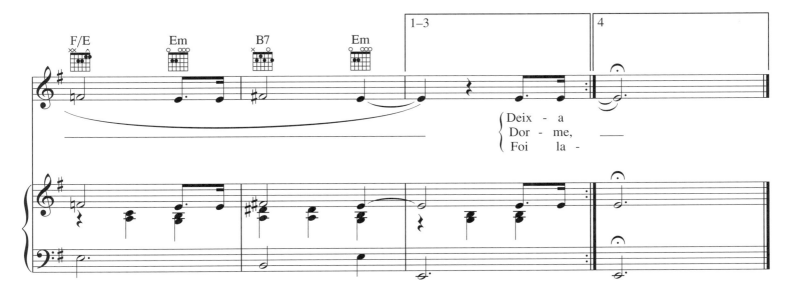

SONG OF THE VOLGA BOATMAN

Russian Folk Song

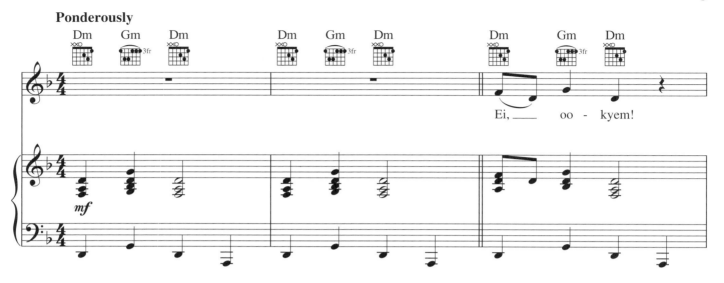

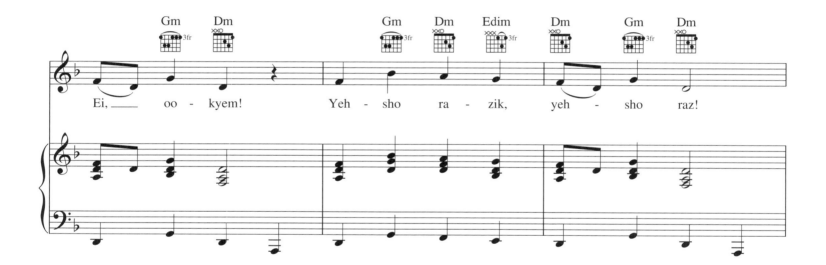

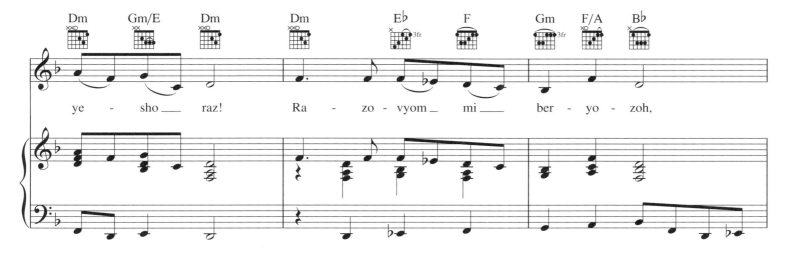

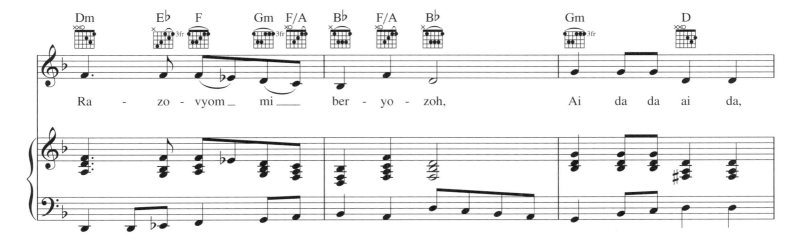

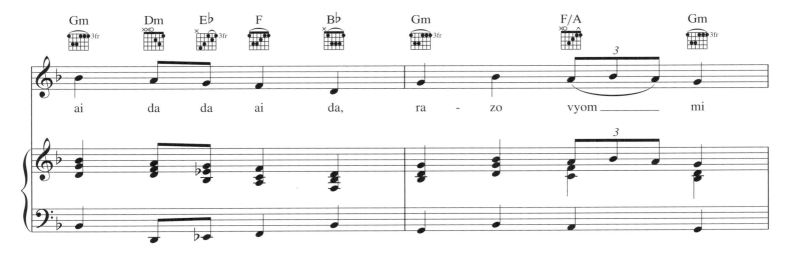

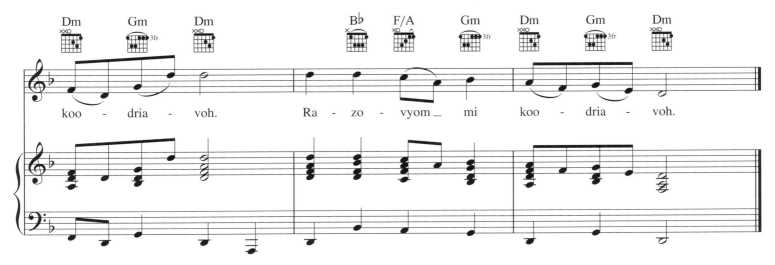

SOSPAN VACH
(The Little Saucepan)

Welsh Folk Song

Moderate March

Mae bys Meri - Ann we - di bri - fo, A

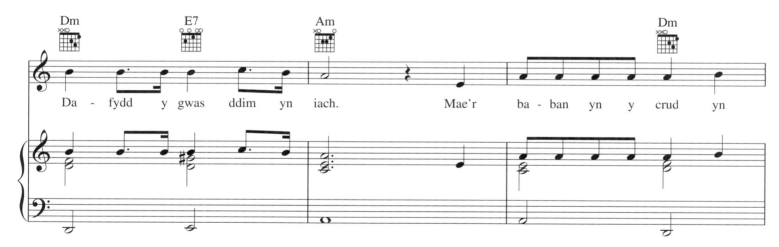

Da - fydd y gwas ddim yn iach. Mae'r ba - ban yn y crud yn

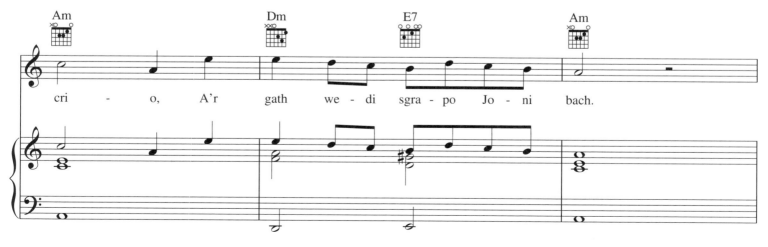

cri - o, A'r gath we - di sgra - po Jo - ni bach.

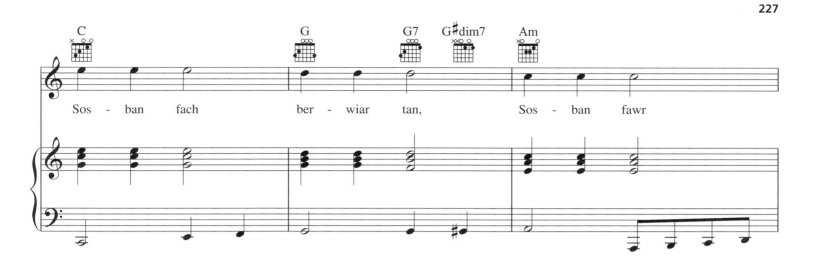

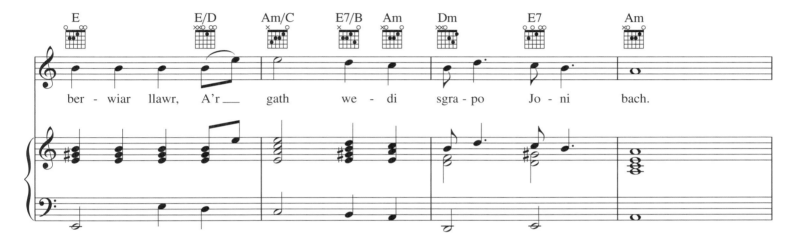

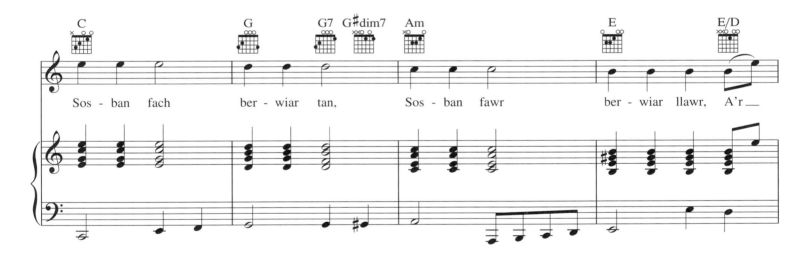

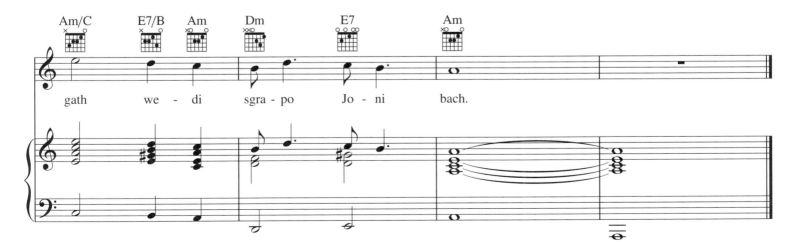

SWING LOW, SWEET CHARIOT

Traditional Spiritual

Moderately

Swing low, sweet

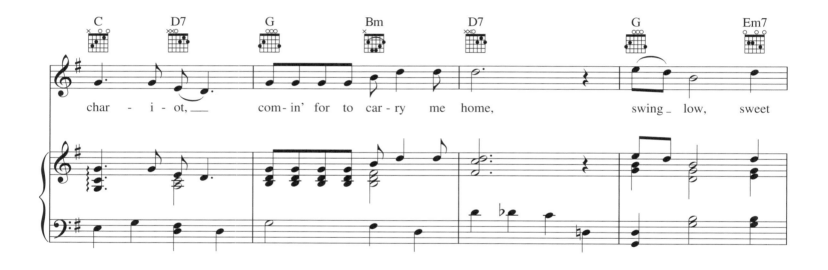

char - i - ot, ___ com - in' for to car - ry me home, swing low, sweet

char - i - ot, ___ com - in' for to car - ry me home. I look o - ver Jor - dan, and

SOMEBODY'S KNOCKING AT YOUR DOOR

African-American Spiritual

Some-bod - y's knock-ing at your door,

some - bod - y's knock-ing at your door,

oh, you sin - ner, why don't you an - swer?
to His teach - ings your heart must o - pen.
Some - bod - y's

knock-ing at your door, could be Je - sus!

door.

SWISS AIR

Traditional

THIS LITTLE LIGHT OF MINE

African-American Spiritual

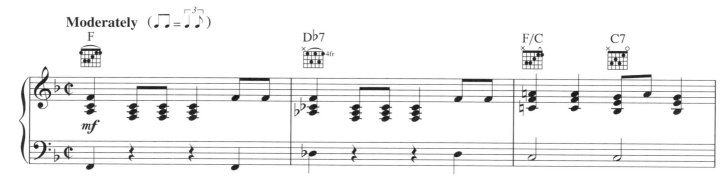

This lit-tle light of mine, ___ I'm gon-na let it shine, ___

___ this lit-tle light of mine, ___

I'm gon-na let it shine. ___ This lit-tle light of mine, ___

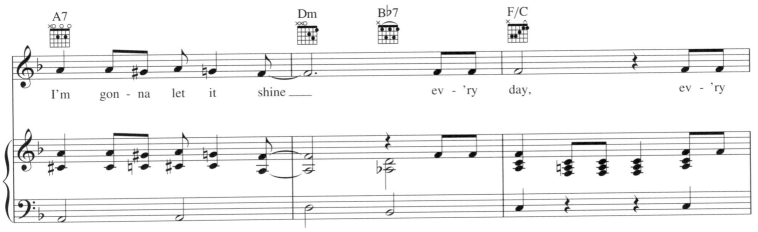

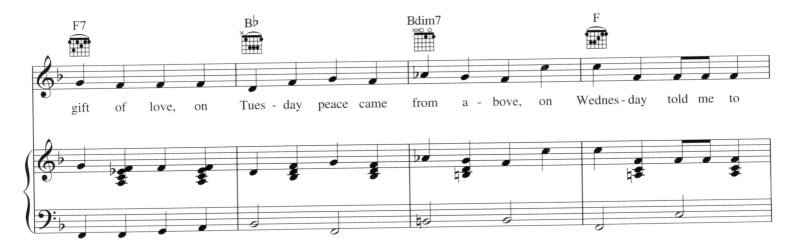

have more faith, on Thurs - day gave me a lit - tle more grace. On

Fri - day told me to watch and pray, on Sat - ur - day told me just

what to say, on Sun - day gave me the pow - er di - vine, just to

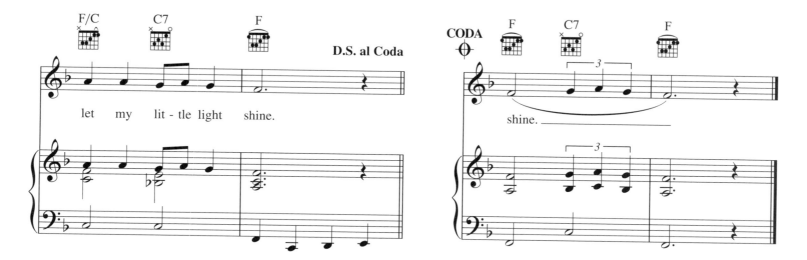

let my lit - tle light shine.

D.S. al Coda

CODA

shine.

THULA THU'
(Hush, Hush)

African Folk Song

THIS OLD HAMMER

African American Work Song

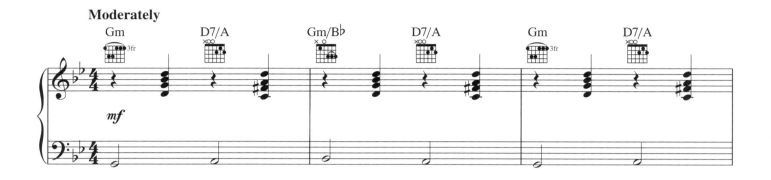

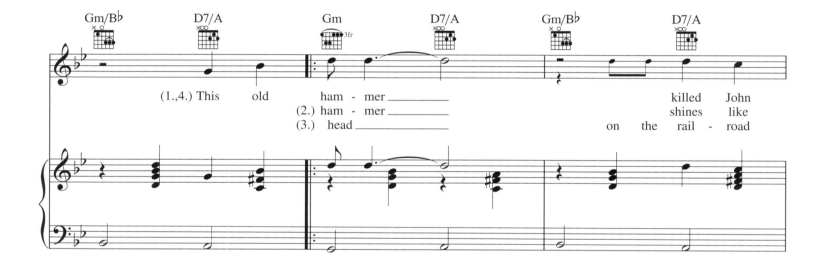

(1.,4.) This old ham-mer _____ killed John
(2.) ham-mer _____ shines like
(3.) head _____ on the rail-road

Hen- ry. _____
sil - ver. _____
track. _____

This old ham- mer _____
This old ham- mer _____
Gon - na lay my head _____

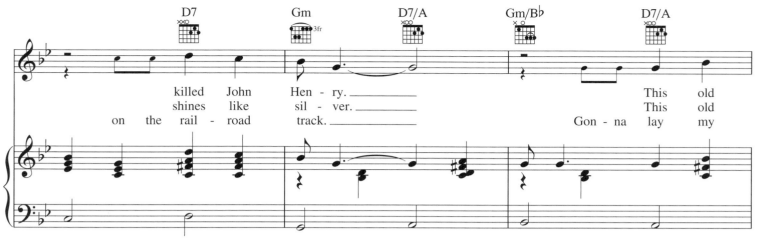

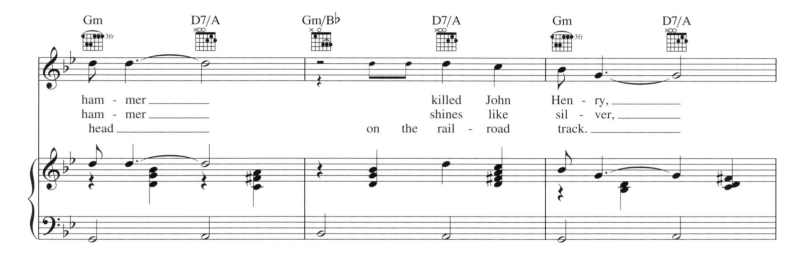

THE THREE RAVENS

Traditional

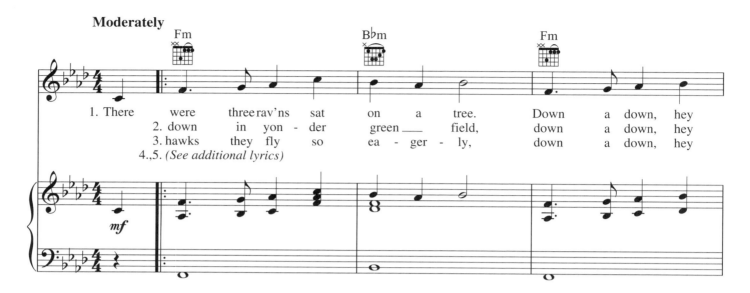

Moderately

1. There were three rav'ns sat on a tree. Down a down, hey
2. down in yon - der green ___ field, down a down, hey
3. hawks they fly so ea - ger - ly, down a down, hey
4., 5. *(See additional lyrics)*

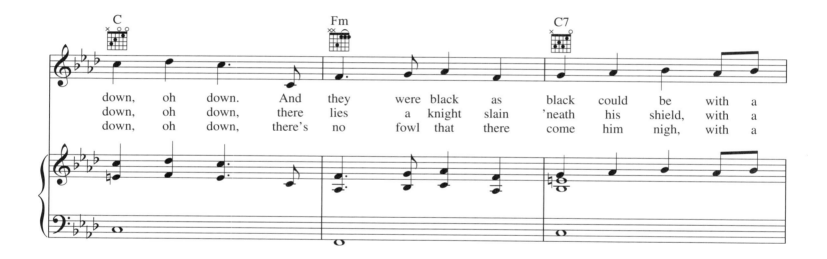

down, oh down. And they were black as black could be with a
down, oh down, there lies a knight slain 'neath his shield, with a
down, oh down, there's no a fowl that there come him nigh, with a

down. ___
down. ___
down. ___

Then one of them said
His hounds they lie down
And down there comes a

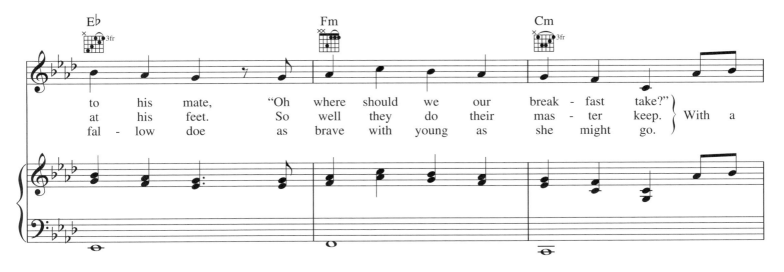

to his mate, "Oh where should we our break - fast take?"
at his feet. So well they do their mas - ter keep. } With a
fal - low doe as brave with young as she might go.

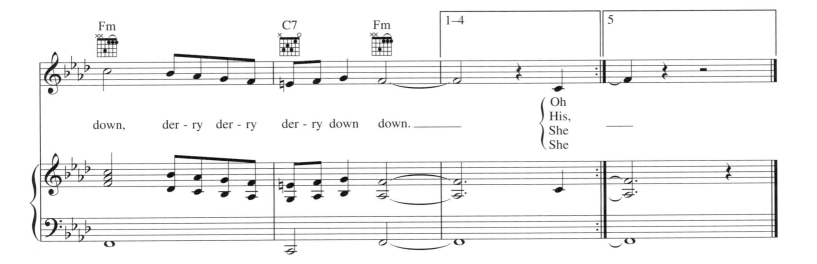

down, der - ry der - ry der - ry down down. _____

Oh
His,
She
She

Additional Lyrics

4. She lifted up his bloody head,
    Down a down, hey down, hey down,
    And kissed his wounds that were so red,
    With a down.
    She got him up upon her back
    And carried him to earthen lake.
    With a down, derry derry derry down down.

5. She buried him before the prime,
    Down a down, hey down, hey down.
    She was dead herself ere even-song time,
    With a down.
    God send every gentleman
    Such hawks, such hounds, and such leman,
    With a down, derry derry derry down down.

TUTIRA MAI

Traditional Maori Folk Song

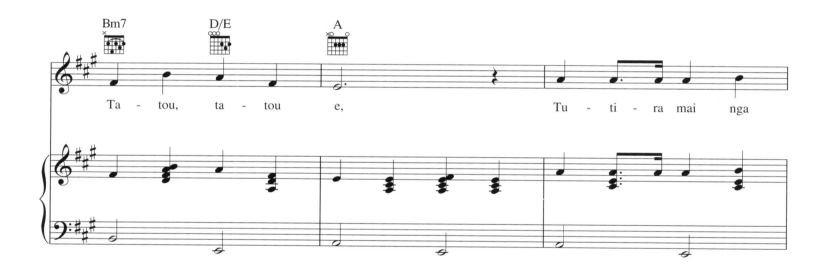

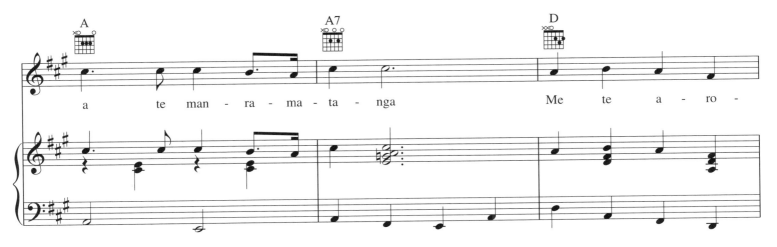

a te man - ra - ma - ta - nga   Me te a - ro -

ha e - nga i - wi ki - a ta - pa - ta - hi ki -

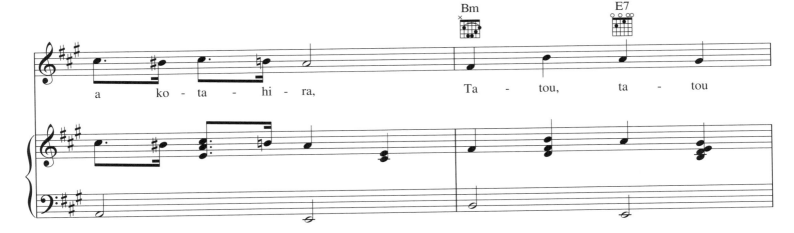

a ko - ta - hi - ra,   Ta - tou, ta - tou

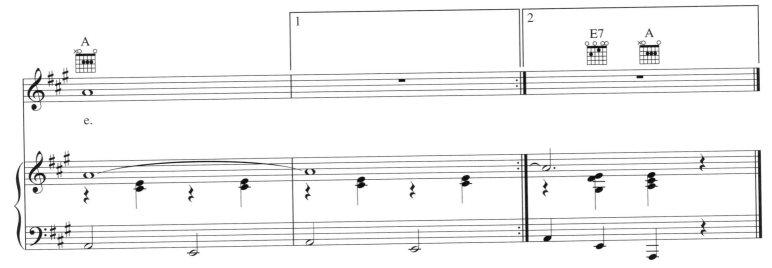

e.

WE GATHER TOGETHER

Words from Nederlandtsch Gedenckclanck
Translated by THEODORE BAKER
Netherlands Folk Melody
Arranged by EDWARD KREMSER

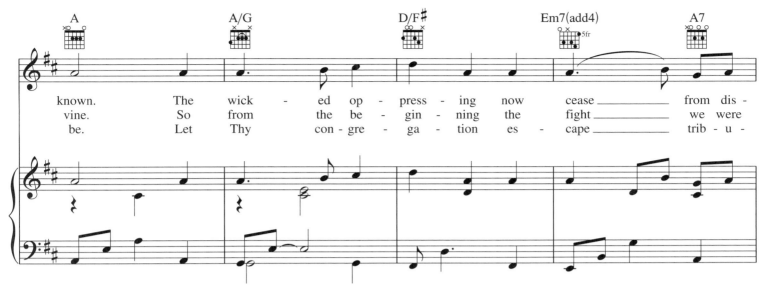

known. The wick - ed op - press - ing now cease _____ from dis -
vine. So from the be - gin - ning the fight _____ we were
be. Let Thy con - gre - ga - tion es - cape _____ trib - u -

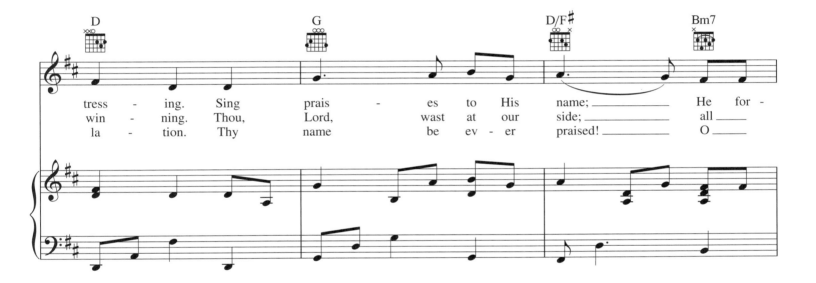

tress - ing. Sing prais - es to His name; _____ He for -
win - ning. Thou, Lord, wast at our side; _____ all _____
la - tion. Thy name be ev - er praised! _____ O _____

gets not His own. Be -
glo - ry be Thine! We
Lord, make us free!

ZUM GALI GALI

Israeli Folk Song

Allegro moderato

Zum Gal - i Gal - i Gal - i Zum Gal - i Gal - i

Zum Gal - i Gal - i Gal - i Zum Gal - i Gal - i. He - cha - lutz le -

a trifle slower

man A - vo - dah   A - vo - dah le - man he - cha - lutz.

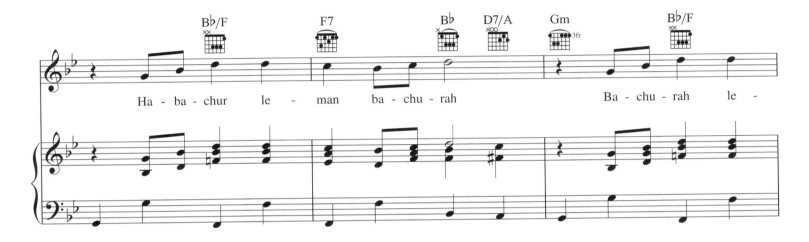

Ha - ba - chur le - man ba - chu - rah   Ba - chu - rah le -

man ha - ba - chur. Zum Gal - i Gal - i Gal - i Zum Gal - i Gal - i

a trifle faster

Zum Gal - i Gal - i Gal - i Zum Gal - i Gal - i.   Zum.

UN LORITO DE VERAPAZ

Guatemalan Folk Song

Moderately

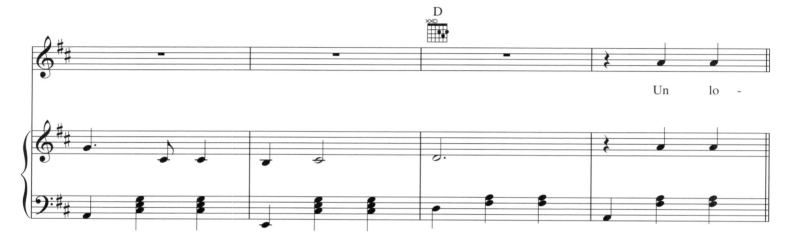

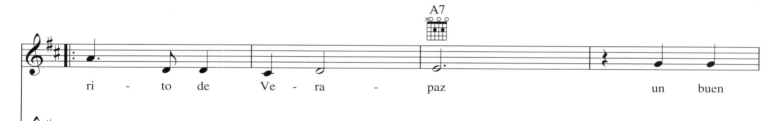

Un lo -

ri - to de Ve - ra - paz un buen

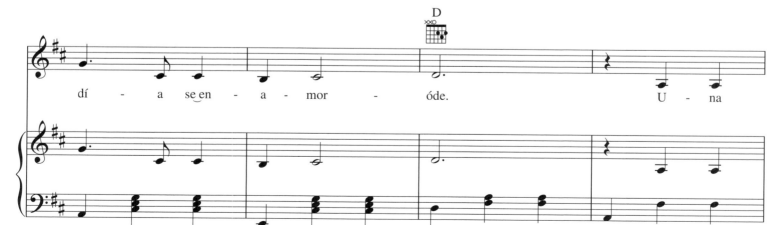

dí - a se en a - mor - ó de. U - na

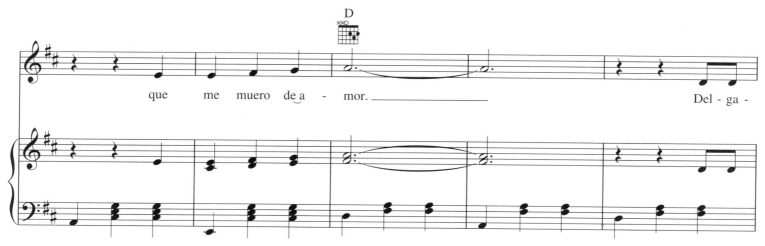

que me muero de a - mor. _____ Del - ga -

di - to me pon - go _____ si tu a - mor no me

das, _____ Si te vas con o - tro ___

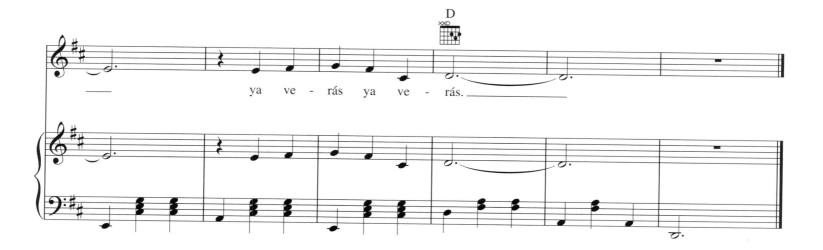

ya ve - rás ya ve - rás. _____